Prop Box Play
50 Themes to Inspire Dramatic Play

Ann Barbour and
Blanche Desjean-Perrotta

Illustrated by Mary Rojas
Cover photograph: Michael Freeman, ©2002

Prop Box Play

50 Themes to Inspire Dramatic Play

Ann Barbour and
Blanche Desjean-Perrotta
Illustrated by Mary Rojas

Gryphon House

Lewisville, NC

Copyright

Copyright © 2002 Gryphon House, Inc.

Published by Gryphon House, Inc.

PO Box 10, Lewisville, NC 27023

Visit us on the web at www.gryphonhouse.com

Illustrations: Mary Rojas

Reprinted August 2016

Library of Congress Cataloging-in-Publication Data

Barbour, Ann.
  Prop box play : 50 themes to inspire dramatic play / Ann Barbour, Blanche Desjean-Perrotta ; illustrations, Mary Rojas.
      p. cm.
Includes index.
  ISBN 978-0-87659-277-9
  1. Play. 2. Early childhood education--Activity programs. 3. Drama in education. I. Desjean-Perrotta, Blanche. II. Rojas, Mary. III. Title.
LB1139.35.P55 B37 2002
372.21--dc21

2002004381

Disclaimer

Bulk Purchase

Gryphon House books are available for special premiums and sales promotions as well as for fund-raising use. Special editions or book excerpts also can be created to specification. For details, contact the Director of Sales at the address above.

Table of Contents

Introduction

Why Play?

"Child's play." Adults often use the term to describe something that is done easily as in, "This is child's play." Indeed, child's play seems to have an effortless quality to it, no doubt because it is spontaneous and natural for most children. Although the term "child's play" may imply that there is "nothing to it" from an adult standpoint, from a child's perspective, it is the opposite. If an adult looks closely at a child during play, she or he will see that play is complex and challenging. It is precisely because play is comprised of a variety of engrossing activities that it is such a rich medium for children's learning and development.

Play is the most important activity of early childhood, the years from birth through age eight. For young children, play is learning. As they play, children acquire and practice new skills and understandings. Play provides a non-threatening context in which children may acquire new concepts, practice evolving skills, and experiment with adult roles without the pressure of conforming to adult expectations. Through play, children are able to set their own goals and carry out their own activities to accomplish those goals. Play supports a child's needs for growth and learning.

A major tenet of early childhood education is that children construct meaningful understandings when they interact with other children and with materials in their environment. Play provides the most important context for these interactions. It supports children's acquisition and refinement of a wide variety of skills and competencies in the areas of social, emotional, cognitive, language, and physical development. Play actively engages their minds and bodies, significantly strengthening the development of the whole child.

Current Trends

Young children in all segments of society have diminished opportunities for play, compared to when their parents or grandparents were children. Changes in demographics result in fewer opportunities to play informally with siblings or other children in the neighborhood. The increase of single-parent and dual-wage-earner homes dictates that children be cared for outside the home and often in structured situations such as after-school programs. The advent of technology and concern for safety outside of the home mean that children spend more time in front of the television or computer than in active play.

The push for early academic achievement, whether to get ready for a particular program or to succeed within one, means that parents and teachers often view play time as time lost to activities they perceive to be more productive. They often regard play and learning as mutually exclusive. As a result, curricula are too often driven by academic standards and accountability measures that preclude play even at the prekindergarten and kindergarten levels. The emphasis on early academics can diminish opportunities for children to play. Some classrooms and early childhood centers give children time to play only after they complete academic assignments. More and more schools and even entire school districts are eliminating recess altogether.

Play is a basic ingredient in every child's care and educational program. Given what we know about the many benefits of play, we can assume that fewer occasions for play result in fewer opportunities for meaningful learning. Teachers and caregivers must find ways to integrate play into programs for young children. One of the easiest ways to do this is to provide time and materials for dramatic play.

Dramatic Play

Dramatic play is pretend or make-believe play where children use objects and roles in imaginative and realistic ways. People who study play believe that group dramatic play, also called sociodramatic play, is the most sophisticated form of play for young children. In sociodramatic play, children think, speak, and act symbolically and in conjunction with others. Each child takes cues from his or her partner in sociodramatic play and responds accordingly. Both dramatic and sociodramatic play provide children with the foundation for a range of skills that will be used later in life. Following is a brief description of the many benefits of dramatic play.

The Benefits of Dramatic Play
Cognitive Development

Engagement in dramatic play positively influences intellectual development. Through dramatic play children learn to:

- represent thought symbolically, a requisite skill for the "3 Rs"
- focus attention and concentrate
- acquire concepts
- hypothesize, test, and revise concepts
- imagine possibilities
- use divergent thinking
- problem-solve
- discover mathematical and scientific concepts (such as classification, seriation, and measurement)
- understand economics

- learn about adult roles and careers
- think strategically
- develop sequential memory

Social and Emotional Development

Peer play provides a rich context for social and emotional development. Through social interactions in play, children come to understand social norms and expectations as well as universal rules that underlie all social interactions. They exercise control in a world that otherwise offers them few such opportunities. In sociodramatic play, children learn to:

- develop friendships
- take turns, cooperate, and share
- listen to others
- share the perspectives of others
- communicate appropriately, both verbally and nonverbally
- collaborate with peers
- negotiate, renegotiate, and resolve conflicts
- adapt behavior to group goals
- explore and express feelings freely
- manage stress
- cope with unrealizable desires
- postpone gratification
- respect themselves and others

Physical Development

Play is the child's primary avenue for physical or motor development, whether the child is developing typically or is physically disabled. Physical activities form an integral part of dramatic play. Within the context of play, children develop and refine their:

- fine and gross motor skills
- balance
- coordination
- eye-hand coordination
- flexibility
- command of their bodies
- perceptual motor development
- spatial and distance awareness
- physical competence and security

Language and Literacy Development

Dramatic play fosters language development at the same time that language supports play. Sociodramatic play stimulates language and literacy development because it incorporates communication, expression, and reasoning. Experiences that are part of children's play benefit children's language and literacy acquisition in a number of ways. In the area of language and literacy, play helps children:

- communicate meaning
- practice conventional speech
- develop narrative language
- create a meaningful environment for the functional use of literacy
- act out stories that enhance story sequence, story sense, and language use
- use situation-specific language (appropriate vocabulary, register, and tone)
- use oral and written language in realistic ways
- use language for critical thinking and problem-solving
- use language to organize and structure activities
- develop various forms of communication
- increase their vocabulary

Creativity

Dramatic play and creativity share many elements. Both rely on a child's abilities to use symbols and complex thinking processes. Children who engage in imaginative play tend to be creative in their approaches to learning and problem-solving. Although creativity is an intellectual process, we have separated it from cognitive development to underscore its importance. With regard to creativity, in dramatic play children:

- express originality in thinking
- explore possibilities
- add to and change the environment in their own ways
- think divergently, generating a variety of responses to different situations
- use both divergent and convergent thinking in the creative process
- make connections between previous experiences
- respond to stimuli in unique ways
- explore and play with ideas
- test and evaluate their skills
- develop an experimental attitude
- develop curiosity (want to know and understand)

Academic Success

With the push to extend academics into early childhood, many educators abandon play because they do not understand its intrinsic value to academic success. Through dramatic play, children develop many of the skills, attitudes, and dispositions necessary for success in a variety of educational settings. When children engage in dramatic play, they:

- enhance their memory
- score higher on tests of imagination and creativity
- develop longer attention spans
- demonstrate involvement in tasks or activities
- cooperate with others
- follow rules
- represent objects and ideas symbolically (a reading skill)
- learn to concentrate
- use symbol systems (a math skill)
- engage in problem-solving
- develop autonomy (self-direction and self-motivation)
- become risk-takers
- practice decision-making
- think imaginatively

The Teacher's Role in Dramatic Play
Creating an Environment

The teacher's primary role in facilitating and supporting dramatic play is preparing the play environment, which can be done before children arrive. Preparing the environment includes arranging the physical space, selecting and gathering props, and displaying them in a way that invites participation. The importance of preparing the environment cannot be underestimated, as it affects children's (as well as teachers') attitudes and behaviors. In early childhood settings, the environment has been called the third teacher (after the teacher and structured activities), with good reason. Room arrangement and materials send powerful messages about what can and should take place in that setting. The environment can either facilitate or thwart children's play experiences.

Time

The amount of time a teacher allows for an activity indicates the extent to which she or he values that activity. Teachers who understand the benefit of dramatic play schedule a sufficient amount of time to allow it to evolve. Large blocks of time are more conducive to dramatic play than short or interrupted time periods. Children need adequate time to choose and negotiate roles, select props, and determine and enact play scenarios. Meaningful sociodramatic play requires at least a 30-minute block of uninterrupted time.

Preparatory Experiences

Children play out what they know. If teachers provide props related to a theme unknown to children, dramatic play will be limited because they have no real-life experience to build on. Teachers may provide background experiences so children can develop dramatic play themes based on common understandings. These preparatory experiences may include primary sources of information such as field trips, visitors, and real artifacts, or secondary sources including literature, stories, videos, museums, photos, and posters. These experiences serve as a springboard for discussion, leading to and supporting children's ideas for dramatic play.

For example, a shoe store theme is likely to be appropriate for all children. However, some children may not have experiences related to pet care. Before introducing play props related to this theme, a field trip to a pet store or veterinarian's clinic is necessary to provide common information for children to use in dramatic play.

Teacher-Child Interactions

Teachers have many roles in supporting children's play. For example, teachers can:

- rearrange the environment to better accommodate play
- supply additional materials to help extend play
- record through photos or dictation what children do in their play
- help children resolve conflicts
- model uses for particular props
- prompt engagement with materials or with others through open-ended questions
- make suggestions about what children can do in their play
- become a co-player

It is important that teachers respect the process of children's play. Children must retain ownership of the play event for a quality play experience to occur. Teachers who are good observers will know which roles best support play without violating children's autonomy and creativity. Careful, thoughtful observation will help teachers understand what children are trying to accomplish in their play. This information will help teachers facilitate play, rather than interrupt or control it.

Creating Dramatic Play Centers

Materials for dramatic play are many and varied. There are no requirements for must-have equipment or materials. Some materials are versatile enough to accommodate different themes and can be used in a variety of ways. Some play equipment can be compared to the pots and pans in a kitchen, which are used daily. In dramatic play, these would be items such as tables and chairs or shelving. In a kitchen, you also find staples such as spices that can be used in a variety of ways, depending on the recipe. It is the same with common props in dramatic play, such as mirrors or baskets. These can be used in a number of ways, depending on the theme, to enhance the appeal of a dramatic play center.

Large Equipment

Large pieces of equipment define the dramatic play space, support small props, and can be modified to become different thematic props. For example, a partition can divide the kitchen and seating area in a restaurant or it can support a lean-to for camping. A low shelf can hold food in a supermarket or it can be turned on its side for a clothes closet. Other versatile pieces of large equipment include:

- peg boards with hooks for hanging hats, clothing, and other props
- low shelves to act as dividers and provide access to props
- an indoor climbing structure that can be covered and converted into a number of structures (space ship, castle, drive-through restaurant window)
- table and chairs
- easel(s) to display signs
- large blocks for children to use to create their own spaces and "furniture"
- a full-length mirror

Small Versatile Props

Versatile props enhance the functionality and appeal of a dramatic play center. The following items support a variety of themes and are good additions to a number of prop boxes:

- blankets
- computer keyboard
- cash register or money box
- dolls

- play money, checkbook, credit cards
- purses and wallets
- eyeglasses without lenses
- clipboard with paper
- telephone
- control panel
- steering wheel
- clothing items that children can manage independently and are not oversized
- baskets and containers of various sizes for organizing small items and for children to use to gather items (e.g., groceries)
- dry erase board and markers
- tape recorder

Print Props

Photographs, pictures, and signs in dramatic play centers make the center more authentic, provide information, help children to make connections between the world outside and inside their classroom, and inspire and extend play. Photos and pictures can be purchased or teacher-made. Children's drawings, artwork, and signs can decorate a center or provide a recorded history of children's play. The following materials can be used to enrich any dramatic play center:

- generic store signs such as Open/Closed or Exit/Enter
- poster board and paper to create signs or posters
- art supplies, such as markers, crayons, glue, scissors, construction paper, modeling clay, or playdough
- camera and film
- sticky notes
- index cards
- file folders

Creating Prop Boxes

What's a Good Dramatic Play Theme?

A good play theme is relevant and of interest to a particular group of children. It should be one with which children are familiar. A rule of thumb is that the younger the children are, the closer to the here-and-now the theme should be. For example, a house theme is relevant and popular with the youngest children because home settings and events that take place in a home and family are familiar to them. Neighborhood store themes (e.g., bakery, gas station) are of interest to older preschoolers and kindergartners. Primary-level children will have an interest in themes related to their expanding understandings of the world, such as a TV production studio, for example.

A good theme supports a variety of role playing and enables children to try on different roles and to interact with others in ways that are consistent with each role. In a restaurant, for example, there are cooks, servers, customers, and a cashier. Through dramatic play, children demonstrate their understandings and skills related to these roles. At the same time, interactions among children playing different roles help them sustain their play, make the play scenario more complex and authentic, and encourage concept and skill development.

Finally, a good play theme is one for which there are readily available primary sources of information as well as opportunities for related experiences. For example, a farm theme is appropriate for children who have an opportunity to visit a farm, speak with a farmer, and see where farm products originate. This theme would be less appropriate where such experiences of this type are not possible.

Which Materials Work Best?

Props are loose parts or accessories that can be placed in a dramatic play center. Open-ended materials that can be used for multiple purposes or are easily transformed make the best prop box materials. Such materials allow children the freedom to express themselves and to exercise

their imagination. Children also need authentic artifacts that are familiar and support their evolving understandings of a particular theme. For example, a child can wear a plain blue shirt as a uniform in a Post Office dramatic play episode, but the child also benefits from having real envelopes, stamps, and postcards to engage in this theme play.

Materials for dramatic play should match the age and developmental needs of the children using them. The younger the child, the more realistic the props should be. For example, a three-year-old needs a real telephone as a prop, but a five-year-old may use a paper tube for a telephone if a real one is not available.

Materials should draw children to play together. Children benefit from sharing their thoughts and feelings with one another about a particular play topic. Props that inspire children to play different roles (doctor and patient or customer and salesperson) teach them to interact with one another. Scrap materials used to construct a house in a construction play center are examples of props that encourage children to play together with a common goal. Materials that children can use simultaneously also work well. For example, a tent encourages children to pretend to camp together. Materials such as these facilitate social and emotional growth.

Materials included in prop boxes should be interesting and engaging in such a way as to encourage and support children's involvement and play.

How Many Props Should There Be?

The number of props depends on the age of the children playing and the theme of their play. Too many props can thwart creativity, overwhelming children with choices. Too few props may be insufficient in inspiring imaginative play. When deciding how many props to include, consider the number of children who will use the props at any given time. In addition, consider the developmental ages of the children involved in play. Younger children may need fewer props but require duplicates. Older children may require more variety but fewer duplicates. Consider the space available to store props. Overstocking a small space can result in a cluttered and unappealing play space. It is better to rotate props or to add a few at a time as children express a need for more.

Supporting Gender and Cultural Inclusiveness

Materials provided for children's play must not perpetuate gender stereotypes. Props boxes should include materials that are attractive to both boys and girls. While some themes may be associated with one gender more than the other—for example, a hair salon or a fix-it shop—a conscious effort should be made to provide props that appeal to both genders. This will make it more likely that all children will find the theme interesting and relevant. Instead of including props associated exclusively with female hair care and beauty products, a hair salon/barber shop prop box should also include shaving cream containers and safety razors (with the blade removed). An easy way to attract girls and boys alike to a dramatic play center is to include clothing for both genders.

Teachers should be sensitive to the unspoken messages that materials convey. If items representative of mainstream culture or a single culture are the only ones included in a prop box, children who are not members of that culture may be subtly excluded from play because they cannot identify with the materials. All brides, for example, do not wear white dresses at their weddings. Chinese brides often wear red. Collecting props representative of a variety of cultures validates the cultural identities of the

children in the group as it expands all children's understanding of the world around them.

This book endeavors to include props that are gender and culture inclusive. Given the diversity of early childhood settings, it is anticipated that individuals using the ideas found in this book will find more ways to support inclusiveness.

Incorporating Literacy and Math Experiences

Opportunities for authentic use of literacy and math skills evolve as children play. Enriching play environments with selected literacy materials encourages children to integrate purposeful reading and writing activities into their play, whatever the theme. During play, children write lists, count money, script stories or letters, measure, weigh, and make labels or signs. Dramatic play is a natural medium for encouraging literacy and math skills. By including props such as writing supplies, books, play money, and measuring tools, teachers convey the message that emerging skills and concepts related to literacy and mathematics are valued and supported. And, children can see that these skills are common and functional parts of everyday life.

Finding Great Props

Most teachers and caregivers have limited funds for dramatic play materials. This need not be a deterrent to supporting dramatic play. Most prop box materials can be made, borrowed, or acquired from garage sales, flea markets, and thrift stores. Businesses often donate items for use in programs for children. Friends, family members, and children's parents are additional sources of prop box materials. Disposable goods such as paper tubes, packing bubbles, Styrofoam peanuts, and coffee cans are easily collected and provide unlimited props in the hands of imaginative children. Thinking of props in terms of flexible use expands resources. A backpack can be a backpack for camping, but it can also be used as a mailbag, a school bag, a tool bag, or a suitcase. Sources for dramatic play materials are limited only by the extent of the teacher's creativity.

Health and Safety Guidelines

Safety is an important consideration when selecting materials for dramatic play. Among the safety factors to consider are whether prop box materials are developmentally appropriate for the age group using them (for example, sharp tools may not be appropriate for some four-year-olds), whether the prop contains toxic materials, if there are any pinch or crush points or sharp edges, and whether there is enough space to use some of the larger pieces of equipment safely. In addition, consider the following when choosing materials for prop boxes and dramatic play:

- materials should not have splinters, loose nuts or bolts, or chipped paint
- painted materials and art materials should be lead-free
- materials that are mouthed should be washed and disinfected between users
- children should not be permitted to play with any type of plastic bag or balloon
- no coins, safety pins, or marbles or items of similar size for children under four years of age
- toy chests to store materials should have air holes and a lid that cannot be locked or no lid at all
- shooting or projectile props should not be used
- props such as rugs, curtains, pillows, blankets, and cloth toys should be flame resistant and should be cleaned periodically
- cords should be removed from clothing (especially from hoods) and appliances (hair dryer, iron, and so on)

- empty containers should be washed thoroughly
- avoid glass items
- do not allow children to share hats and combs and similar items if there is a problem with head lice in the group, or simply remove these items from the prop box

Be aware of any messages these materials convey to children. For example, substituting candy for pills in an empty medicine bottle may prompt some children to associate medicine with candy. If children have been exposed to substance abuse, syringes may be all too familiar. In these instances, teachers may choose not to include these props.

Storage Suggestions

Props gathered for each dramatic play theme can be stored in easy-to-stack sturdy cartons with lids. Some larger props can also be used as storage containers. For example, a suitcase can hold the materials for the airplane prop box. Label prop boxes for quick identification. As additional materials are collected, they are easily added to existing prop boxes. Include a list of the contents on the outside of the container. Items that are too large to fit in the container should also be listed so they are not overlooked when the dramatic play center is set up.

Using This Book

Selecting a Prop Box

The following pages include ideas for assembling 50 different prop boxes. This is by no means an exhaustive list, as children's play can generate many more themes depending upon their background and interests. Prop boxes can enhance a larger theme study, introduce an idea or concept, or build on children's curiosity about a particular topic. Two or more prop boxes can be combined to complement one another. For example, a bakery prop box and a birthday prop box can be used together. Children can bake and sell pastries in the bakery center for use in a birthday celebration center.

Although there are 50 prop boxes listed, the intention is not that they be used on a weekly rotating basis. Children's interests and engagement with materials should determine when a prop box is used and how long it is used.

Guide to Prop Box Format
Basic Props

Each of the prop boxes lists basic props. While it is not necessary to include every item, the props in this list are easily obtainable and sufficient to start a dramatic play center.

When clothing or food items are listed as props or are part of related activities, care should be taken to ensure that these items are culturally appropriate for the children who will use them.

Additional Props

Ideas for additional/supplemental props that support the theme and encourage children to extend and elaborate play are included. Teachers can select items from this list as they deem necessary or as time and financial resources allow.

Vocabulary

Dramatic play with authentic materials and other children provides a natural context for vocabulary development. Vocabulary words for items or concepts related to the theme are listed for each prop box. Teachers can introduce these words as children play, augmenting the literacy experiences inherent in dramatic play.

Extension Activities

A list of ideas for learning activities related to the theme of each prop box is included. Some are more suitable for preschool and kindergarten, others for first and second grade. Use your knowledge of children's abilities and interests to select appropriate activities. These activities can easily be adapted to individual situations.

Unless otherwise indicated, activities should be done by the children or by the children and teacher together.

Related Literature

Any theme can be enriched through reading well-chosen literature. This book lists an assortment of picture books (written for preschool to primary-age children) that can be read to or with children or made available to them in the dramatic play area or classroom library. Select books that match the abilities and interests of the children in your class.

Whenever possible, the book lists include multicultural literature. However, in some instances, books providing diverse cultural perspectives related to a theme are either limited or do not exist. Many of the children's books listed are translated into Spanish and can be found in libraries or through Internet searches.

Prop Boxes

Airplane Prop Box

Vocabulary

aisle
altitude
arrival
baggage
beverage
cabin
coach
cockpit
copilot
departure
destination
distance
exit
first class
flight attendant
ground crew
landing
luggage
meal service
passenger
pilot
safety procedures
security
speed
suitcase
take off
travel agent
turbulence
velocity
x-ray

Basic Props

Airline tickets
Books, games, and other items for carry-on bags
Carry-on bags
Earphones/headsets
Flight attendant uniforms (shirt with drawn-on insignia)
Instrument panel (See directions in Appendix, page 124.)
Magazines
Pilot's microphone (See directions in Appendix, page 125.)
Pilot uniforms (hat and/or shirt with drawn-on wings)
Plastic cups
Safety pamphlets

Additional Props

Breathing apparatus (See directions in Appendix, page 121.)
Flags (to help park planes)
Food cart (box with wheels attached)
Flight schedule
Life jacket
Metal detector (foil-wrapped paper tube)
Pillows and blankets
Plastic trays, dishes, cutlery
Small suitcase
Steering wheel
Travel brochures
Travel items (clothing, toiletries, pajamas)
Windows (blue paper ovals with cotton ball clouds, covered with plastic wrap)
Window shade or chart paper for movie screen

Extension Activities

- Take a trip to the airport. Visit the ticket counter, gate, and baggage area.
- Invite a pilot or flight attendant to visit the class.
- Provide materials for children to make and decorate paper airplanes.
- Make a list with the children of items to pack for a trip.
- Fold large pieces of construction paper in half to make suitcases. Children can draw items inside their suitcase on the paper.
- Children can paint pictures of the view from an airplane on window-shaped paper. Display in the dramatic play area.
- Plan an itinerary for a trip with children. Plot the route on a map with yarn and pushpins.

- Play "Red Light, Green Light" (see Appendix, page 127) on the playground in an area marked as a runway. Children can "fly" with their arms outstretched only when the air traffic controller gives them the signal.

Related Literature

Airport by Byron Barton
All Aboard Airplanes
  by Frank Evans
Amelia's Fantastic Flight
  by Rose Bursik
Angela's Airplane
  by Michael Martchenko
Christopher's Little Airplane
  by Mark S. James
Flying by Donald Crews
First Flight
  by David M. McPhail
Gila Monsters Meet You at the Airport by Marjorie Weinman Sharmat
Going on a Plane
  by Anne Civardi
I Fly by Anne F. Rockwell
Magic School Bus Taking Flight: A Book About Flight
  by Gail Herman

Archeologist Prop Box

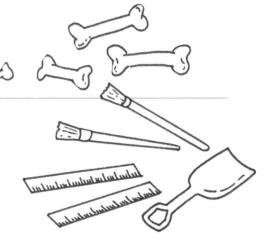

Vocabulary

ancient
archeology
area
artifact
assemble
buried
classify
date
dig
discover
earth
excavate
fossil
history
locate
mummy
pyramid
reconstruct
sample
shard
sift
uncover

Basic Props

Backpacks
Boots
Hats
Magnifying glass
Maps
Neckerchief/bandana
Notebook
Objects for discovery (large dog biscuits for bones, pieces of broken clay pottery, rocks, miniature pots, marbles, and so on)
Sand strainer
Sunglasses
Tools (little shovels, brushes, rulers, hammer, and so on)

Additional Props

Archeological magazines
Baggies
Camera
Canteen
Dolls and gauze to make mummies
Drawing tools
Florist stones for gems
Microscope
Pictures/posters of dinosaurs

Pith helmet
Posters/pictures of pyramids/mummies
Small rakes and shovels
Tape measure
Various-size brushes for cleaning artifacts

Extension Activities

- Bury objects in the sand table or sandbox and let children dig and discover.
- Watch a video about archeological digs and discoveries.
- Invite a guest archeologist to explain his/her work to the class.
- Place objects for discovery outdoors and invite children to go on an archeological expedition.
- Supply different-sized dog biscuits in the shape of bones and have children measure and record the sizes.
- Use a dinosaur model that comes apart and bury the bones in a sandbox. Have children find the bones and then construct the model just like archeologists do.

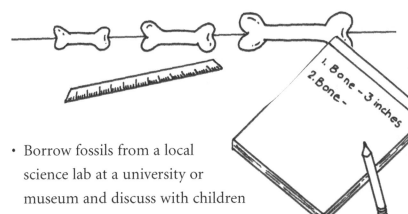

- Borrow fossils from a local science lab at a university or museum and discuss with children how these were formed. Then have them create their own fossils using clay and seashells.
- Create artifacts to bury and find using clay or playdough (recipe in Appendix, page 129).
- Create a snack and have children dig to find it. Snack ideas include M&Ms buried in chocolate pudding; an edible pyramid made of Jell-O blocks; or a mummy made from a gingerbread man cookie wrapped in marshmallow.
- Write a song about digging to the tune of "A Hunting We Will Go."
- Purchase sand of different colors and have children layer the sand in a baby food jar, creating original designs.

Related Literature

And Still the Turtle Watched by Sheila MacGill-Callahan

Big Old Bones: A Dinosaur Tale by Carol Carrick

Danny and the Dinosaur by Syd Hoff

Fossils Tell of Long Ago by Aliki

How Do Dinosaurs Say Goodnight? by Jane Yolen and Mark Teague

I Am the Mummy Heb-Nefert by Eve Bunting

The Magic School Bus in the Time of the Dinosaurs by Joanna Cole

The Magnificent Mummy Maker by Elvira Woodruff

Patrick's Dinosaurs by Carol Carrick

Time Flies by Eric Rohmann

Time Train by Paul Fleischman

What Happened to Patrick's Dinosaurs? by Carol Carrick

The Worry Stone by Marianna Dengler

Architect Prop Box

Vocabulary

addition
angle
blueprint
client
construction
create
design
distance
drafting
engineer
entrance
function
imagine
improvement
landscape
measure
model
pattern
plan
proportion
protractor
renovation
roof
room
scale
skyscraper
space
structure
support
wall

Basic Props

Assorted pencils and pens
Blueprints
Clipboards
Erasers
Graph paper
Pictures of buildings and houses
Rulers
Scissors
String (for measuring or tying to pencils to make protractors)
Wooden blocks

Additional Props

Colored pencils
Compass
Drafting board
Foam core pieces to build with
Glue
Hard hat
Pager
Protractors
Safety glasses
T-square
Tape
Telephone
Triangle
Yardstick

Extension Activities

- Tour a building site accompanied by the architect.
- Take a neighborhood walk. Identify different shapes in buildings. Record the number of squares, rectangles, circles, and so on for comparison.
- Measure the length of a building in footsteps and then in feet.
- Draw a room at home or the classroom to scale, using graph paper. Label rooms and/or special features.
- Design a structure on the computer using appropriate software (for example, *Blocks in Motion*).
- Use a blueprint to plot the actual size of a house or building on the playground.
- Construct buildings from scrap wood or pieces of foam core using children's architectural drawings.
- Draw a bird's-eye view of the playground from the top of a climbing structure.
- Ask children to write a description of their house or apartment building.
- Make models of houses and other buildings by taping together playing cards or index cards.

Related Literature

Arches to Zigzags: An Architecture ABC
  by Michael J. Crosbie
Building a House
  by Byron Barton
Ésta Es Mi Casa
  by Arthur Dorros
Everyday Structures from A to Z
  by Bobbie Kalman
The House Book
  by Keith Duquette
A House for Hermit Crab
  by Eric Carle
How a House Is Built
  by Gail Gibbons
Homes Around the World
  by Bobbie Kalman
Houses and Homes
  by Ann Morris
My House by Lisa Desimini
Roberto, the Insect Architect
  by Nina Laden

Bakery Prop Box

Vocabulary

bagel
batter
biscuit
chewy
cookie
decorate
dough
equivalent
flour
frosting
gooey
ingredients
knead
liquid
loaf
muffin
pancake
pastry
quantity
recipe
shortening
sticky
tablespoon
teaspoon
temperature
tortilla
yeast

Basic Props

Aprons
Bowls
Cake pan
Cash register or money box
Cookbook with photos
Cookie cutters
Cookie sheet
Empty ingredient containers (baking powder, flour, and so on)
Hand mixer (with cord removed)
Measuring cups and spoons
Play money
Price list (dry-erase board and pen)
Receipt book
Timer
Wooden spoons

Additional Props

Bags
Bakers' hats (See directions in Appendix, page 121.)
Cake decorations (buttons, ribbon, lace, yarn, and so on)
Eggbeater
Hand towel
Flour sifter
Garlic press (to use with playdough)
Muffin tin
Pastry bag
Pie tin
Plastic knives
Playdough (See recipe in Appendix, page 129.)
Potholders
Rolling pin
Scale
Spatula
Tortilla press
Whisk

Extension Activities

- Substitute pre-made bread dough and flour for playdough.
- Visit a bakery. Point out baked goods, displays, workers' jobs, and price lists.
- Help children follow a recipe to make bread, pretzels, or muffins.
- Help children bake bread with and without yeast and compare the results.
- Share favorite types of bread with family members.
- Taste and compare different kinds of bread products.

- Stir one package of dry yeast into a cup of warm water. Encourage children to describe what they observe over the course of several hours.
- Add measuring spoons and cups to a sensory table filled with flour or playdough. Record equivalencies by drawing or writing.
- Decorate small cupcakes or muffins with frosting or cream cheese to which food coloring has been added. Let children "sell" these in the bakery before snack time.

Related Literature

Bakers Make Many Things
  by Carol Greene
Bread, Bread, Bread
  by Ann Morris
Bread Is for Eating
  by David Gershatar
Bruno the Baker
  by Lars Klinting
Everybody Bakes Bread
  by Norah Dooley
The Giant Jam Sandwich by
  John Vernon Lord and Janet
  Burroway
Hedgehog Bakes a Cake
  by Maryann MacDonald
Knead It, Punch It, Bake It!
  by Judith and Evan Jones
The Little Red Hen
  by Paul Galdone
*This Is the Bread I Baked for
  Ned* by Crescent Dragonwagon
Tony's Bread: An Italian Folktale
  by Tomie dePaola
The Tortilla Factory
  by Gary Paulsen

Bank Prop Box

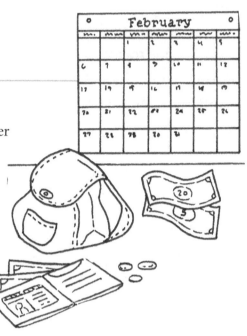

Vocabulary

account
ATM
banker
budget
cashier
change
check
credit
deposit
dime
dollar
earn
heads/tails
loan
nickel
overdraft
owe
penny
quarter
receipt
safety deposit box
save
security
spend
teller
withdraw

Basic Props

Bank book
Calendar
Cash register or money drawer
Checks
Deposit/withdrawal slips
Wallets, purses
Money
Old credit or bank cards
Pens/pencils
Rubber stamps
Telephone

Additional Props

ATM machine (See directions in Appendix, page 121.)
Banner with bank name
Computer or keyboard
Drive-up window (See directions in Appendix, page 123.)
Items for safe deposit box (jewelry, photos, certificates,
    documents, and so on)
Plastic tube for drive-up deposit
Safety deposit boxes (tissue boxes)
Sign with banking hours

Extension Activities

- Visit a local bank.
- Have children earn play money in class and show them how to open a savings account.
- Use the bank in class as part of a reward system.
- Provide materials that children can purchase by taking loans from the bank.
- Discuss and role play different jobs at the bank.
- Provide a game where children have to match price tags to the exact change pictured on cards.
- Fill a jar with pennies and challenge children to estimate the amount, and then count to check.
- Talk with children or read with them about the people whose pictures are found on paper currency.

Related Literature

26 Letters and 99 Cents
   by Tana Hoban
Alexander Who Used to Be Rich Last Sunday by Judith Viorst
Arthur's Funny Money
   by Lillian Hoban
Arthur's TV Trouble
   by Marc Brown
Bunny Money by
   Rosemary Wells
Four Dollars and Fifty Cents
   by Eric A. Kimmel
The Hundred Penny Box
   by Sharon Mathis
Lemonade for Sale by
   Stuart Murphy
Little Bunny's Cool Tool Set
   by Maribeth Boelts
What Zeesie Saw on Delancey Street by Marjorie Priceman
The Wishing Hat
   by Annegert Fuchshuber
Yard Sale by James Stevenson

Beach Prop Box

Vocabulary

breakers
clam
crab
coast
coral
driftwood
float
fog
island
lake
lifeguard
lighthouse
motor boat
ocean
sailboat
sand castle
sand dune
seagull
seaweed
seashell
shore
snorkel
sunburn
sunscreen
surf
tide
tide pool
vacation
wave

Basic Props

Books and magazines
Bucket, shovel, trowel
Flippers
Goggles
Lifeguard log-in book
Red lifeguard shirt
Sandcastle molds

Sandals
Sunglasses
Sun hats
Sunscreen bottle
Seashells
Swimsuits/trunks
Towels

Additional Props

Beach bag
Beach ball
Beach chairs
Binoculars
Ice chest
Kickboard
Magnifier
Piece of driftwood
Sand sifter
Shells for Sale sign

Shore or wildlife field guide
Signs (Lifeguard, No
   Swimming, and so on)
Sun visor
Swim caps
Toy boats
Umbrella
Water wings
Water/soda bottles

Extension Activities

- Take a trip to the beach or to a local aquarium.
- Group children into small groups to paint a mural of the seashore.
- Encourage children to draw or write with their fingers in a shallow tray filled with sand.
- Invite a lifeguard to come in and talk about water safety.
- Examine different kinds of sand with magnifying glasses.
- Add water and a variety of plastic containers to the sand on the playground so children can make sandcastles.
- Give children large pieces of cardboard shaped like small surfboards and paint to create their own "boogie boards."
- Bury seashells in the sand and water table for children to find, sort, and classify.
- Sample different kinds of food from the sea, such as tuna sandwiches, fish fingers, and sushi (rice wrapped in seaweed).

Related Literature

At the Beach by Anne and Harlow Rockwell

At the Beach by Huy Voun Lee

Beach Ball by Peter Sis

Beach Day by Karen Roosa

Beach Play by Marsha Hayles

A Day at the Beach by Mircea Vasiliu

Henry and Mudge and the Forever Sea by Cynthia Rylant

Just Grandma and Me by Mercer Mayer

The Puddle Pail by Elisa Kleven

Sea, Sand, Me! by Patricia Hubbell

The Seashore (A First Discovery Book) by Gallimard Jeunesse, et al

The Seashore Book by Charlotte Zolotow

See You in Second Grade by Miriam Cohen

Those Summers by Aliki

When the Tide Is Low by Sheila Cole

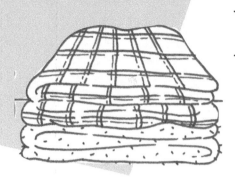

Bedtime Prop Box

Vocabulary

bedspread
bedtime
blanket
bunk bed
ceiling
comfortable
constellation
cot
cozy
dawn
dream
drowsy
dusk
evening
giants
midnight
monsters
morning
nap
night
nightmare
pretend
quilt
routine
scary
shadow
sheet
silhouette
sleepy
stars
twilight

Basic Props

Blankets
Clock
Flashlights
Pajamas
Pillows
Storybooks
Stuffed animals

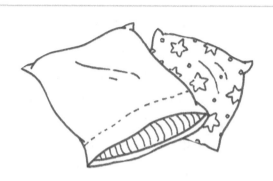

Additional Props

Alarm clock
Bathrobes
Dolls
Inflatable mattress
Nightlight
Plastic cup
Sleeping bag
Slippers
Table lamp
Toothbrush
Washcloth and towel

Extension Activities

- Create monsters from assorted two- and three-dimensional materials.
- Talk about bedtime fears.
- Darken the windows with black or blue paper punched with small holes for stars.
- Hold a pajama day where everyone, including teachers, comes to school dressed in sleepwear.
- Provide sticky stars, black paper, and light-colored crayons so children can create a nighttime sky.

- Have children vote whether Ira in *Ira Sleeps Over* should or should not get the teddy bear. Place the votes in a box and then count and record.
- Ask children to keep a log, either describing or drawing, of the moon's changing shape. Draw the moon over several weeks.
- Turn out the lights and read a bedtime story by flashlight.
- Have children cover their eyes and try to identify various objects by sound.
- Make crayon etchings by solidly covering a sheet of paper with a variety of colors. Color over this with a dark crayon (black, blue, purple) and then etch a design in it by scraping it with a Popsicle stick, plastic knife, or fork.
- Make hand shadows in front of a flashlight.
- Ask children, with parents' help, to record their bedtimes for one week.
- Using plastic overlays and grease pens or markers, encourage children to draw a nighttime monster. They can place these over the pages in the book *There's a Nightmare in My Closet*.

Related Literature

Bedtime for Frances
   by Russell Hoban
Can't You Sleep, Little Bear?
   by Martin Waddell
Goodnight Moon by Margaret
   Wise Brown
Grandfather Twilight
   by Barbara Berger
Hush! A Thai Lullaby
   by Minfong Ho
Ira Sleeps Over by Bernard Waber
The Napping House
   by Audrey Wood
Night Noises by Mem Fox
Owl Moon by Jane Yolen
*There's a Monster Under My
   Bed* by James Howe
*There's an Alligator Under My
   Bed!* by Mercer Mayer
*There's a Nightmare in My
   Closet* by Mercer Mayer
Time for Bed by Mem Fox
Time to Sleep
   by Denise Fleming

Birthday Party Prop Box

Vocabulary

age
attend
birthday
calendar
candle
card
celebration
congratulate
decoration
favor
friendship
frosting
gift
greeting
guest
host
invitation
manners
month
place setting
plan
preparation
present
reply
RSVP
special occasion
surprise
thank-you note
wrap
year

Basic Props

Birthday candles
Birthday crown
Camera
Cake (See directions in Appendix, page 122.)
Candles
Ice cream scoop
Ice cream container
Invitations
Plastic plates, cups, and utensils
Party hats
Tablecloth and napkins

Additional Props

Dolls
Dress-up clothes
Cake-making materials (bowl, spoon, eggbeater, egg carton, cake mix box, pastry bag, and so on)
Empty boxes (gifts)
Favors
Happy Birthday sign
Index cards to make birthday cards, place cards, or invitations
Piñata
Pitcher
Playdough (See recipe in Appendix, page 129.)
Numbers to put on cake
Ribbons or stick-on bows
Wrapping paper and tape

Note: Minimize consumable props (wrapping paper, paper napkins) as much as possible to minimize expense and save time replenishing them.

Extension Activities

- Mark each child's birthday on the calendar.
- Create a birthday bulletin board for each month. Display baby and recent photographs of children whose birthdays fall in that month.
- Wrap familiar objects (block, cup, pencil, and so on) in wrapping paper. Ask children to guess what's inside.
- Create a matching game by gluing different pieces of wrapping paper to two index cards each.
- Ask children to put the correct number of birthday candles on pictures of cakes labeled with different numerals.
- Provide materials for children to make a gift and/or a birthday card for a family member, friend, pet, or stuffed animal.
- Have children make and decorate party hats.
- Play traditional birthday games (Pin the Tail on the Donkey, drop clothespins in a bottle, Ring-Around-the-Rosie, sack race, three-legged race, egg-on-a-spoon race, and so on).
- Bake cupcakes following a recipe or frost and decorate prepared cupcakes.
- Ask children to calculate the number of items needed to set the table for a certain number of guests.
- Put 1 tablespoon of white frosting in each cup of a Styrofoam egg carton. Have children mix food coloring into the frosting to create different colors.
- Place 4-6 gift boxes of various sizes and the same number of pieces of wrapping paper on a table. Ask children to match the smallest box with the smallest piece of paper and so on. Help children wrap the boxes and then place them in order from smallest to largest.
- At the beginning of each month, give children with birthdays that month paper strips to create birthday chains. Each child's chain should have the same number of links as his or her birth date (for example, 24 links for March 24th). Hang up the chains. Children can count down to their birthdays by removing one link each day.
- Ask children to brainstorm birthday gifts beginning with each letter of the word "birthday." Record their suggestions on chart paper.

Related Literature

Alfie and the Birthday Surprise
   by Shirley Hughes
Arthur's Birthday
   by Marc Brown
Ask Mr. Bear by Marjorie Flack
Benjamin's 365 Birthdays
   by Judi Barrett
A Birthday for Frances
   by Russell Hoban
Birthday Presents
   by Cynthia Rylant
Come to My Party
   by Emilie Barnes
Happy Birthday
   by Gail Gibbons
Happy Birthday, Moon
   by Frank Asch
Horray, a Piñata!
   by Elisa Kleven
A Letter to Amy
   by Ezra Jack Keats
Moira's Birthday
   by Robert Munsch
Night Noises by Mem Fox
The Seven Silly Eaters
   by Mary Ann Hoberman
Will It Ever Be My Birthday?
   by Dorothy Corey

Camping Prop Box

Vocabulary

backpacking
campfire
campsite
compass
conservation
constellation
dawn
dehydrated food
desert
direction
dusk
environment
forest
gear
habitat
hike
lantern
moonlight
mountain
national park
nature
necessities
park ranger
prepare
protection
provisions
supplies
trail
wilderness
wildlife

Basic Props

Backpack
Baseball hats
Binoculars (See directions in Appendix, page 121.)
Camera
Campfire (See directions in Appendix, page 122.)
Flashlight or lantern
Map (purchased or teacher-made)
Pots and pans or mess kit
Plastic plates and utensils
Sleeping bag or rolled blanket tied with string
Sunglasses
Warm clothing (jackets, hats, and so on)

Additional Props

Cards or small game board
Compass
Empty bottles of sunscreen
Empty food packages
Field guide books
First aid kit
First aid manual
Fishing pole
Flyswatter
Frying pan
Mugs
Rain jacket or poncho
Small cooler
Spatula
Sun hats
Tent or blanket draped over rope
Thermos

Extension Activities

- Darken the windows with black or blue paper with punched-out holes for stars.
- Sing songs while sitting around the campfire.
- Give children a trail map to follow as they hike around the playground, or have them follow a trail of crumbs to find something interesting (for example, a stuffed bear) at the trail's end.
- Ask children to write about or draw a camping adventure.
- Invite a park ranger to talk about camping, caring for the environment, and safety.
- Make trail mix with children and eat it for snack. (See recipe in Appendix, page 130.)
- Give children natural materials (leaves, twigs, pine cones, pebbles, and so on) to use to create collages.
- Discuss with children items needed for an overnight camping trip. Make a list of their suggestions on chart paper. Ask them to create or bring to school any items on the list that are not included in the dramatic play center.

Related Literature

Amelia Bedelia Goes Camping
  by Peggy Parish
Arthur's Camp-Out
  by Lillian Hoban
Backpacking by Jimmy Holmes
Bailey Goes Camping
  by Kevin Henkes
Curious George Goes Camping
  by Margaret and H.A. Rey
Just Camping Out
  by Mercer Mayer
The Lost Lake by Allen Say
Monk Camps Out
  by Emily Arnold McCully
My Camp-Out
  by Marcia Leonard
Sleep Out by Carol Carick
Three Days on a River in a Red Canoe by Vera B. Williams

Castle Prop Box

Vocabulary

apprentice
armor
castle
coat-of-arms
crown
defend
dragon
drawbridge
dungeon
jester
keep
king
knight
lord
magician
medieval
moat
prince
princess
protection
queen
royal
scepter
scroll
shield
tournament
wizard

Basic Props

Adult shirt with a sash or belt for knight's tunic
Crowns/tiaras
Jester hat (See directions in Appendix, page 124.)
Material for capes
Old dresses and scarves
Old jewelry
Princess hats (See directions in Appendix, page 127.)
Scrolls made from paper towel rolls
Shields (made from heavy cardboard)
Toy stick horses (See directions in Appendix, page 128.)

Additional Props

Artificial food and dishes
Baton for jester (dowel decorated with ribbon and bells)
Black material for wizard's cape
Fancy clothing, lacy material
Green cloth for dragon
Knight's helmet (See directions in Appendix, page 124.)
Long garden gloves
Musical instruments
Poster of castle (from travel agency)
Royal cups (decorated plastic wine cups)
Royal scepters (See directions in Appendix, page 127.)
Trumpet
White cloth and a rolled paper cone that can be worn
  for a unicorn
Wizard's hat (See directions in Appendix, page 129.)
Wizard's wand (dowel with star at one end)

Extension Activities

- Have children create a coat-of-arms for the shields.
- Make a face mask for the dragon.
- Build a castle with wooden blocks.
- Visit a local armory museum.
- Reenact a fairy tale with a castle theme, such as *Snow White, Sleeping Beauty, Jack and the Beanstalk,* or *Cinderella.* Videotape it so children can revisit the play.
- Provide a game where children match pairs using only the face cards from a deck of cards.
- Have "royal tarts" for snack (pop tarts or frosted cookies).
- Invite parents to share pictures of castles they have visited in their travels, and scan them into a computer so children can visit them, too..
- Read *Jack and the Beanstalk.* Have children germinate some lima beans.
- Have a fairy tale ball at the castle. Have children design invitations. Dress up for the ball.

Related Literature

Adventures of the Little Green Dragon by Mari Privette Ulmer

Castles: A First Discovery Book by Claude Millet Jeunesse, C. Delafosse, C. Millet, and D. Millet

The Dragon's Pearl by Julie Lawson

The Dragon's Scales by Sarah Albee

I Am Really a Princess by Carol Diggery Shields

Into the Castle by June Crebbin

The Knight and the Dragon by Tomie dePaola

Knights in Shining Armor by Gail Gibbons

The Knight Who Was Afraid of the Dark by Barbara Shook Hazen

The Paper Bag Princess by Robert Munsch

The Paper Dragon by Marguerite W. Davol, et al

Princess Jessica Rescues a Prince by Jennifer Brooks

The Royal Nap by Charles C. Black

Sarah's Unicorn by Bruce and Katherine Coville

The Selfish Giant by Oscar Wilde and Katrien Van Der Grient

Circus Prop Box

Vocabulary

acrobat
animal tamer
applause
audience
balance
big top
circus
clown
fortune
highwire
juggler
megaphone
microphone
names of circus animals
performance
performer
ringmaster
rings
tightrope
trapeze
stunt
train

Basic Props

Animal print cloth for circus animals
Circus tickets
Clown clothing (wigs, hats, large shoes, gloves, rubber balls with
    hole for nose, clown masks, adult shirts in fun prints, adult
    pants cut down, suspenders, and so on)
Ears and tails for circus animals
Face paint for clowns
Microphone (glue a Ping-Pong ball on one end of a paper tube
    and spray paint)
Stuffed animals
Tall hat for ringmaster
Tights and decorated T-shirts

Additional Props

A 2" x 4" length of wood for tightrope walker
Ball for fortune-teller
Ballet shoes and costume
Bathing suits for acrobats
Circus posters
Clown hats made from rolled paper cones
Flyers announcing arrival of circus
Hula hoops for circus rings or for animals to jump through
Large cloth to hang between two chairs or over a table for a tent
Megaphone made of rolled cardboard
Mustache for ringmaster
Play money
Popcorn/boxes
Small umbrella for tightrope walker
Tape on the floor for tightrope
Tapes of animal sounds
Tennis balls to juggle

Extension Activities

- Discuss the different jobs in a circus.
- Create a poster for the circus.
- Locate the schedule of a real circus on the Internet and follow its movements on a map.
- Explain the purpose of clown school and how each clown's face is a personal signature. Create clown faces.
- Watch popcorn pop. Have popcorn for snack.
- Have a popcorn race by blowing popcorn kernels across a table.
- Have a circus day outdoors where each child can perform.
- Make up silly fortunes to tell each other when acting as a gypsy fortune-teller.
- Create props for the circus such as tickets, posters, and masks.
- Provide materials to make a lion's mask using a paper bag. Children cut holes for eyes and glue yarn on the bag for the mane.

Related Literature

Circus by Lois Ehlert
Circus Family Dog by Andrew Clements, Sue Truesdell
The Circus Surprise by Ralph Fletcher
Circus Train by Joseph Smith
Clown by Quentin Blake
Emeline at the Circus by Marjorie Priceman
Felix Joins the Circus by Annette Langen, et al
Ginger Jumps by Lisa Campbell Ernst
If I Ran the Circus by Dr. Seuss
Just Clowning Around by Steven MacDonald
Marvin the Tap-Dancing Horse by Betty Parashwas
Mirette on the High Wire by Emily Arnold McCully
Oliver by Syd Hoff
Star of the Circus by Mary Beth Sampson
When the Circus Came to Town by Polly Horvath

Construction Prop Box

Vocabulary

addition
architect
blueprint
cabinet
carpenter
cement
construction
electrician
engineer
entrance
foundation
frame
improve
join
measure
plan
plumber
remodel
rebuild
repair
roof
safety
site
sturdy
tool names (drill,
  hammer, pliers, clamp,
  and so on)
wall
wiring
woodwork

Basic Props

Assorted tools (hammer, screwdriver, plane, and so on)
Boxes and small building supply scraps
Clipboard and paper
Dropcloth
Hardhats
Ruler
Safety goggles
Scrap wood (Note: Sand to prevent splinters.)
Screws
Styrofoam pieces with golf tees to nail
Tape measure
Work gloves
Work shirts

Additional Props

Blueprints
Bucket
Calculator
Canvas utility aprons
Carpenter's pencil
Clamps
Flashlight
Level
Paintbrushes

Paint rollers
Paint swatches
Paint trays
Plastic cones
Sandpaper
Shovel
T-square
Walkie-talkie

Extension Activities

- Arrange for a construction worker to come in and demonstrate uses of tools and other materials.
- Visit a construction site. Children can carry clipboards to draw/record what they observe.
- Plan a woodworking activity incorporating items from the prop box.
- Give children paintbrushes and buckets of water to "paint" playground equipment or an outside wall.
- Use different measuring devices (ruler, yardstick, folding ruler, tape measure, T-square, and so on). Discuss which ones make it easier or harder to measure particular items.
- Place a tree stump, hammer, and nails outside for children's use. Supervise carefully.
- Make collages using wood shavings, colored telephone wires, and so on.
- Place a variety of sizes of nuts and bolts on a tray. Children can screw pairs together.

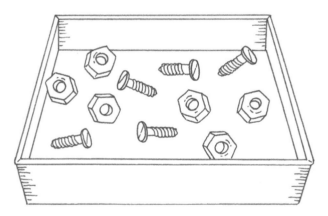

- Sing "This Is the Way . . ." ("we saw the wood," "paint the wall," and so on).
- Draw plans for a building and then build the building out of blocks.
- Discuss and demonstrate tool safety.
- Put children in small groups. Together they can construct a building out of boxes, paper rolls, empty packaging, corks, straws, screen, and so on. Spray paint the completed structure. Ask children to tell or write about features of the structure.

Related Literature

Big Builders by Susan Korman

Building a House by Byron Barton

A Busy Day at the Building Site by Phillippe Dupasquier

Construction Site (Who Works Here?) by Lola M. Schaefer

Construction Workers by Tami Deedrick

How a House Is Built by Gail Gibbons

Mr. Paul and Mr. Lueke Build Communities (Our Neighborhood) by Alice K. Flanagan

The Night Worker by Kate Banks

Those Building Men by Angela Johnson

Tool Book by Gail Gibbons

Tools by Ann Morris

The Wilsons, a House-Painting Team (Our Neighborhood) by Alice K. Flanagan

Cowboy/Cowgirl Prop Box

Vocabulary

bandana
bedroll
branding iron
bronco
brand
bridle and bit
bunkhouse
cattle
chuck wagon
contestant
corral
graze
hay
herd
horseshoe
lasso
livestock
nugget
prairie
ranch
range
reins
rodeo
saddlebags
spurs

Basic Props

Bandanas
Cowboy/cowgirl hats
Short lengths of rope
Sieves to pan for gold
Small blankets rolled up and tied with string used as bedrolls
Small rocks painted gold
Stick horses
Stuffed animals to rope
Teacher-made animal masks (cows, horses, pigs, and so on)
Western boots
Western posters

Additional Props

Artificial cactus
Audiotape of Western music or farm animal sounds
Bales of hay
Bolo (string tie)
Canteen
Chaps
Chuck wagon (fold a piece of white stiff cardboard over a child's wagon)
Corral fencing
Horseshoes
Long underwear
Marshal's badge
Rodeo posters
Saddle bags
Saddle tossed over bale of hay
Vests
Winner medals/ribbons
Wood logs (for artificial camp fire)

Extension Activities

- Teach children a Western line dance.
- Explain how each piece of Western clothing has a distinct purpose (for example, bandanas are used for washing, straining drinking water, as a dust mask, and as a tourniquet for first aid).
- Explain the purpose of branding, and have children create their own special brand.
- Give children large pieces of thick string and show them how to braid a rope.
- Have a cattle roping contest outdoors using stuffed animals.
- Create an imitation campfire (use logs and flashlights) and eat snack or lunch around the campfire while singing songs or telling tall tales. (Don't forget to turn off the overhead lights!)
- Create a Western mural as a backdrop for the class, painting in cactus and mountains.
- Display a variety of real cactus plants.
- Place small rocks painted gold in a bucket. Let children use sieves to pan for gold.
- While outdoors, children pretend to be on a cattle drive using stick horses and stuffed animals.
- Make bolo ties using plastic lacing and large buttons, which can be painted.
- Prepare an authentic ranch lunch of chili, baked beans, cornbread, and punch.
- Brainstorm a list of chores to be done on a ranch and each child can role play one chore.
- Use the grocery store prop box to make a General Store.
- Have a Western-wear day where everyone wears jeans and a bandana.

Related Literature

Armadillo Rodeo by Jan Brett

The Cowboy and the Black-Eyed Pea by Tony Johnston

Cowboy Dreams by Dayal Kaur Khalsa

Cowboy Small by Lois Lenski

Cowboys by Glen Rounds

Cowgirl Rosie by Stephen Gulbis

The Cowgirls by Joyce Gibson Roach

The Golly Sisters Go West by Betsy Byars

Just Like My Dad by Tricia Gardella

Matthew the Cowboy by Ruth Hooker

Rodeo by Cheryl Walsh Bellville

Sam's Wild West Show by Nancy Antle

Why Cowboys Sleep with Their Boots On by Laurie Lazzaro Knowlton

Yippee-Yay: A Book About Cowboys and Cowgirls by Gail Gibbons

Dentist Prop Box

Vocabulary

anesthetic
appointment
braces
cavity
check-up
crown
decay
enamel
filling
floss
gargle
gums
hygienist
incisor
molar
names of different teeth
    (incisors, molars,
    cuspids, bicuspids, and
    so on)
plaque
prevention
receptionist
root
swish and spit
tooth decay
toothache
x-ray

Basic Props

Appointment book or dry-erase board
Bowls
Calendar/notepad
Empty mouthwash bottles filled with water
Floss
Paper bibs
Paper cups
Popsicle sticks
Posters of teeth
Small flashlight
Telephone
Tooth mirror
Toothpaste/toothbrushes
White shirt

Additional Props

Dolls
Face mask
False teeth
Models of teeth
Money/checks/credit cards
Old dental x-rays
Puppets with mouths that open
Rubber gloves

Extension Activities

- Draw a smile and glue in the right number of "teeth" (white popcorn kernels).
- Sing familiar songs using new words, such as "This is the Way We Brush Our Teeth."
- Invite a dentist to bring the tools used in a dentist's office and discuss their uses with the children.
- Using a large model of teeth, discuss dental hygiene.
- Demonstrate with children how to floss using floss and an egg carton turned upside down for teeth.
- Count your teeth with your tongue.
- Make a tooth bag from scraps of material to put under the pillow for the tooth fairy.
- Use a food chart to discuss foods that help bones and teeth to grow strong.
- Bring in a variety of toothpastes. Have children taste each one and chart their preferences. See which toothpaste is most popular.
- Research which other living things have teeth. Make a list.
- Eat a snack of fruits and crunchy vegetables that help clean teeth.
- Create a collage of foods that are good for or bad for teeth.

Related Literature

Andrew's Loose Tooth
  by Robert Munsch
Arthur Tricks the Tooth Fairy
  by Marc Tolon Brown
Dear Tooth Fairy by Kath
  Mellentine and Tim Wood
Grandpa's Teeth by Rod Clement
Just Going to the Dentist
  by Mercer Mayer
Milo's Toothache by Ida Luttrell
Mr. Sugar Came to Town
  by Harriet Rohmer and
  Cruz Gomez
My Dentist Makes Me Smile
  by Leslie Craig
Nice Try, Tooth Fairy
  by Mary W. Olson and
  Katherine Tillotson
Open Wide: Tooth School Inside
  by Laurie Keller
Rosie's Baby Tooth
  by Maryann Macdonald
*Throw Your Tooth on the Roof:
  Tooth Traditions from Around
  the World* by Selby B. Beeler
The Tooth Book by Theo Lesieg
  and Joseph Mathieu
Trevor's Wiggly-Wobbly Tooth
  by Lester Vaminack

Detective Prop Box

Vocabulary

case
clue
conclude
crime
discover
disguise
evidence
examine
fingerprint
identification
incognito
information
investigate
law
locate
magnify
monocle
mystery
observation
search
secret code
sleuth
solve
trail
uncover
walkie-talkie

Basic Props

Boy's and girl's dress
shirt/blouse
Camera
Flashlight
Hat
Jackets
Latex gloves
Magnifying glass

Maps
Message pad
Notebook
Scarf and tie
Sunglasses
Telephone
Watch or clock

Additional Props

Baby powder and brush (to dust for clues)
Briefcase
Disguise materials (mustache, wig, and so on)
Inkpad and paper (to make fingerprints)
Monocle
Plastic glasses with nose attached
Sherlock Holmes pipe
Telescope
Walkie-talkie

Extension Activities

- Provide clues for children to follow in order to locate their snacks.
- Write a message with disappearing ink. Dip a fine brush in lemon juice or vinegar. Place paper on warming tray or hold close to a light bulb to see the message.
- Develop a secret code where one letter stands for another and send a message to a friend in code.
- Invent a mysterious occurrence (for example, a classroom item disappears). Give children verbal or written clues or leave evidence (such as chalk dust on the windowsill for a missing chalk eraser) to help them solve the mystery.
- Make thumb and fingerprint creations. Draw faces and bodies on fingerprints.
- Provide several kinds of magnifying glasses for children to use. As they compare differences, guide them to discover the concept of magnifying power.

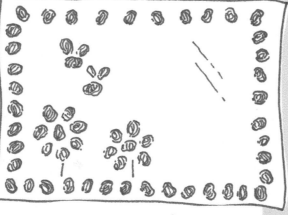

- Set up an outdoor scavenger hunt. Give children a list of things to find.
- Use index cards to make detective business cards.

Related Literature

Berenstain Bears and the Missing Dinosaur Bone by Stan and Jan Berenstain

Detective Dinosaur by James Scofield

The Eleventh Hour: A Curious Mystery by Graeme Base

Gumshoe Goose by Mary Deball Kwitz

Jane Martin, Dog Detective by Eve Bunting

Lights, Camera, Clues! by Carolyn Keene

Marty Frye, Private Eye by Janet Tashijan

Only the Cat Saw by Ashley Wolff

Owly by Mike Thaler

Richard Scarry's Best Mysteries Ever! by Richard Scarry

The Soccer Shoe Clue by Carolyn Keene

Somebody and the Three Blairs by Marilyn Tolhurst

What's the Matter, Davy? by Brigitte Weninger

Whoo-oo Is It? by Megan McDonald

Why a Disguise? by David McPhail

Doctor Prop Box

Vocabulary

appointment
bandage
body parts
cast
check-up
care
cure
disease
doctor
emergency
first-aid
germ
heal
healthy
hospital
illness
injury
medicine
nurse
operation
patient
prescription
splint
stethoscope
stitches
surgery
thermometer
tongue depressor
treatment
vaccination
wound

Basic Props

Baby dolls
Bandages/tape
Blanket
Blunt scissors
Clipboard with medical
  history forms
Cotton balls
Empty pill bottles

File folders
Lab coat (old white shirt)
Money/checks/credit cards
Prescription pads
Scarves for slings
Stethoscope
Telephone
Tongue depressors

Additional Props

Appointment book
Cotton swabs
Crutches
Doctor's medical bag
Human body chart
Growth chart
IV drip (paper cups suspended
  with yarn)
Latex gloves
Magazines/books for a
  waiting room
Medical masks

Nurse's cap
Old x-ray films (or teacher-
  made on transparency sheet)
Patient gowns
Reflex hammer
Scales (baby and adult)
Thermometers
Tubes/bottles of hand cream
Typewriter
Wagon for ambulance
Wet wipes

Extension Activities

- Invite healthcare professionals to visit and explain their jobs.
- Trace children's bodies so they can draw their internal organs, such as heart and stomach and lungs. Or, provide pre-drawn pictures of organs to cut and paste.
- Have children practice dialing the emergency number 911.
- Have children run in place and teach them how to find their pulse.
- Have children create a book about staying healthy with pictures of themselves eating good foods, exercising, and getting rest.
- Put empty syringes in the water table for children to practice filling.
- Role play with children what happens when you visit the doctor.
- Discuss safety related to taking medicine (for example, never take medicine without adult supervision).
- Have two children weigh themselves and add the two weights together, or chart children's weight and have them guess who is the heaviest, lightest, and so on.

Related Literature

Arthur's Chicken Pox
  by Marc Tolon Brown
The Berenstain Bears Go to the Doctor by Stan and Jan Berenstain
A Button in Her Ear
  by Ada Bassett Litchfield
Chris Gets Ear Tubes
  by Betty Pace
Clifford Visits the Hospital
  by Norman Bridwell
Disney's Winnie the Pooh: Pooh Gets a Checkup by Kathleen W. Zoehfeld
Dr. White by Jane Goodall
Elmo Goes to the Doctor
  by Sarah Albee
Franklin Goes to the Hospital
  by Sharon Jennings
Going to the Hospital
  by Fred Rogers, et al
Hola, Doctor by David Marx
Miffy in the Hospital
  by Patricia Crompton
My First Doctor's Visit
  by Julia Allen
Phil and Lil Go to the Doctor
  by Rebecca Gold
Who's Sick Today?
  by Lynne Cherry

Entomologist Prop Box

Vocabulary

chrysalis
cocoon
colony
egg
entomologist
feelers
helpful/harmful
hive
larvae
metamorphosis
names of common insects
  (ants, butterflies, moths,
  bees, grasshoppers, flies,
  wasps, termites, earwigs,
  and so on)
nectar
parts of insects (head,
  thorax, abdomen,
  antennae, wings, legs,
  eyes, proboscis, stinger,
  and so on)
pest
pollen
pollinate
roles of insects
  (queen, worker, drones,
  scouts, and so on)
spin
web

Basic Props

Crickets or mealworms (can be purchased at pet store)
Insect identification book
Insect pictures
Magnifying glass
Paper/pencil/markers
Plastic jars with screwtop lids for bug specimens
Tweezers
White shirt, adult size

Additional Props

Abandoned hives or sample hives from a beekeeper
Ant farm
Beekeeper hat (attach a piece of netting to a baseball cap)
Binoculars
Butterfly farm (purchased)
Butterfly nets
Clipboard
Cricket habitat (See directions in Appendix, page 122.)
Gloves
Ladybugs (can be purchased at a nursery)
Live plants and flowers
Microscope
Petri dishes
Yellow T-shirt painted with black stripes and a headband with
  pipe cleaner antennae

Extension Activities

- Explain the different roles of bees in hives (queen, drones, and workers). Have children act out the work that goes on in a beehive, assigning different jobs to the children.
- Go on a bug hunt, and demonstrate careful collection of specimens.
- Make paper butterfly wings and have children pretend to sip nectar during outdoor play.
- Make feelers by attaching pipe cleaners to headbands. Children can pretend to be part of an ant colony acting out the different roles (nest builder, food gatherer, scout, caretaker of young, and queen) or march and sing "The Ants Go Marching One by One."
- Enjoy a snack made from insect products, such as honey!
- Pretend to be grasshoppers. Have a jumping contest to see who can jump the farthest.
- Invite a beekeeper or entomologist to come in and speak about studying and working with insects.
- Plant a butterfly garden outside the classroom window and watch for visitors.
- Invite children to bring specimens from their own backyard to add to the laboratory.
- Tell riddles about bugs.
- Imitate cricket sounds using rhythm sticks.
- Give children magnifying glasses and clipboards. Investigate insect habitats such as a flower garden, meadow, seashore, or marsh. Have children draw what they see.
- Purchase or create an ant farm to observe.

Related Literature

The Bee Tree by Patricia Polacco
Billy's Beetle by Mike Inkpen
The Girl Who Loved Caterpillars: A Twelfth Century Tale from Japan by Jean Merrill
Grasshopper on the Road by Arnold Lobel
The Grouchy Ladybug by Eric Carle
In the Tall, Tall Grass by Denise Fleming
Miss Spider's Tea Party by David Kirk
Old Black Fly by Jim Aylesworth
Ten Flashing Fireflies by Philemon Sturges
Two Bad Ants by Chris Van Allsburg
The Very Hungry Caterpillar by Eric Carle
The Very Lonely Firefly by Eric Carle
The Very Quiet Cricket by Eric Carle
When the Fly Flew In by Lisa Westberg Peters
Why Mosquitos Buzz in People's Ears: A West African Tale by Verna Aardema

Farm Prop Box

Vocabulary

barn
barnyard
crop
farm equipment names
fruit and vegetable names
harvest
haystack
hoe
irrigate
kinds of farmers: dairy,
   beef, fruit
livestock
names of farm animals
organic
plant
plow
poultry
produce
reaper
silo
tractor

Basic Props

Animal ears, noses, tails
Bandanas or neckerchiefs
Child-size farm tools
Corn or hay to feed animals
Feeding instructions
Hoe
Pail
Rake
Sign with name of farm
Straw hat
Stuffed animals
Toy farm trucks
Work shirts

Additional Props

Audiotapes of animal sounds
Award ribbons (for County Fair)
Baskets
Bib overalls
Packages of flower seeds
Pail to milk cows
Plastic eggs
Plastic fruits and vegetables
Samples of local produce
Small bags of hay

Extension Activities

- Create a barn using a large refrigerator box.
- Place small plastic farm animals in the block play area. Use blocks to create stalls and fences.

- Bake cornbread or make carrot salad for snack.
- Take a field trip to a farm or farmer's market.
- Discuss how food gets from farm to market.
- Plant seeds and watch them grow (use rapid-growing radish seeds).
- Play the "The Farmer in the Dell."
- Use small plastic fruit baskets as stalls, label each stall with a number, and have the children place the appropriate number of small plastic animals in the stalls.
- Choose a name and design a sign for the farm.
- Make farm animal masks.
- Play "Pin the Tail on the Farm Animals."
- Make a barn diorama using shoeboxes filled with paper animals that children have colored and cut out.
- Paint with buttermilk on black paper.
- Pretend to milk cows. (See directions in Appendix, page 125).
- Sort farm animals from non-farm animals.

Related Literature

Barnyard Banter
   by Denise Fleming
Big Red Barn
   by Margaret Wise Brown
Click, Clack, Moo: Cows that Type by Doreen Cronin
The Cow that Went Oink
   by Bernard Most
The Crippled Lamb
   by Max Lucado
Farm Alphabet Book
   by Jane Miller
Farmer Duck
   by Martin Waddell
A Farmer's Alphabet
   by Mary Azarian
Good Morning, Chick
   by Mirra Ginsburg
Hooray for Orchards
   by Bobbie Kalman
The Little Red Hen
   by Paul Galdone
No Milk!
   by Jennifer A. Ericsson
Petunia by Roger Duvoisin
Pigs from A to Z
   by Arthur Geisert
Tractor Mac by Billy Steers

Favorite Stories Prop Box

Goldilocks and the Three Bears, The Three Little Pigs, Little Red Riding Hood

Vocabulary

character
collapse
construction
directional terms (in, on top of, under, next to, and so on)
disguise
escape
fantasy
fool
forest
hardness words (soft, medium, hard, and so on)
manners
material
outsmart
plan
porridge
pretend
rescue
scare
size relation words (small, medium, large, and so on)
stray
sturdy
temperature words (hot, warm, cool, cold, and so on)
trespass
trick

Basic Props

Goldilocks' wig (See directions in Appendix, page 123.)
Papa Bear's hat (See directions in Appendix, page 124.)
Mama Bear's wig with headband and bear ears
Baby Bear's baseball cap with cardboard bear ears attached
3 bowls of different sizes
3 spoons
3 different cushions
Red cape
Basket
Wolf ear headband (See directions in Appendix, page 120.)
Grandma's cap
Blanket
3 sets of pig ear headbands (See directions in Appendix, page 120.)

Additional Props

Apron
Clothing for characters
Construction worker's vest
Cooking pot
3 pillows of various degrees of softness
Plastic food
House fronts from large cardboard boxes to simulate straw, wood, and bricks
House materials (straw, sticks, and blocks)
Wolf nose or mask
3 pig noses or masks

Extension Activities

- Provide materials for children to make props, such as masks or headbands.
- Encourage children to act out their own fairy tales for others.
- Retell fairly tales using flannel board figures.
- Use straws, sticks, and small blocks to build houses.

- Sort a variety of items by size, hardness, weight, or length.
- Make and eat porridge (oatmeal, cream of wheat, or cream of rice) for snack. Use a thermometer to measure the temperature of cold porridge, hot porridge, and "just right" porridge.
- Read several versions of the same story. Discuss and list differences.
- Discuss the meaning of make-believe and/or fairy tales. Show videos of wolves, pigs, and bears in their natural habitats.

Related Literature

Goldilocks and the Three Bears
    by James Marshall
Goldilocks and the Three Bears
    by Jan Brett
*Goldilocks and the Three Bears;
    Bears Should Share! (Another
    Point of View)* by Alvin
    Granowsky, et al
Hog-Eye by Susan Meddaugh
*Leola and the Honeybears: An
    African-American Retelling of
    Goldilocks and the Three Bears*
    by Melodye Benson Rosales
Little Red Riding Hood
    by Trina Schart Hyman
*Little Red Riding Hood: A
    Newfangled Prairie Tale* by
    Lisa Campbell Ernst
*Lon Po Po: A Red-Riding Hood
    Story from China* by Ed Young
The Three Little Cajun Pigs
    by Berthe Amoss
*Three Little Hawaiian Pigs and
    the Magic Shark* by Donivee
    Laird
The Three Little Javalinas
    by Susan Lowell
*The Three Little Pigs: An Old
    Story* by Margot Zemach
*The Three Little Pigs and the
    Fox: An Appalachian Tale* by
    William H. Hooks
*The True Story of the 3 Little
    Pigs!* by Jon Scieszka
The Wolf Is Coming!
    by Elizabeth MacDonald

Fire Station Prop Box

Vocabulary

911
aerial ladder
alarm
axe
bravery
ember
emergency
extension ladder
fire extinguisher
fire hydrant
fire hose
firefighter
fire prevention
helmet
hook and ladder
hose
hydrant
nozzle
paramedic
rescue
safety
siren
smoke detector
stepladder
stop, drop, and roll
stretcher

Basic Props

Black garden boots
Blocks to build houses
Cellophane or streamers for fire
Fire safety brochures (free at fire station)
Firefighter hats (purchased, or see directions in Appendix, page 123)
Old rubber hose (cut into 4' lengths)
Rubber garden gloves
Street map
Telephone (to call 911)
Toy fire trucks

Additional Props

Artificial food and dishware
Axes (cut out of cardboard)
Bell (for siren or firehouse alarm)
Dolls to be rescued from the house (male/female and representative of the ethnicity of the children in the group)
Gurney (See directions in Appendix, page 123.)
Large cardboard box (house) painted with red flames
Red, orange, and yellow cellophane cut into flames
Stuffed dog (Dalmatian or a white dog marked with black bingo marker spots)
Toy fire trucks
Used smoke detector
Yellow child-size raincoat

Extension Activities

- Take a field trip to a fire station or watch the video *Sesame Street Visits the Firehouse.*
- Have children practice calling 911.
- Discuss how to "stop, drop, and roll" in case of fire and have the children role play.
- Explain the value of a smoke detector in a home.
- Discuss what firefighters do when they are waiting in the firehouse (sleep, eat, play games).
- Talk about fire safety (for example, don't play with matches).
- In warm weather, play with water hoses using the playground superstructure as the "house on fire."
- Make ladders for snack using licorice sticks or pretzel sticks and peanut butter.

- Pretend straws are fire hoses and drink through the "hose."
- Use a real ladder to teach the concepts of over, under, and through.
- Show children how fire needs air to burn using a candle in a glass jar and a lid.

Related Literature

Barney and B.J. Go to the Fire Station by Mark S. Bernthal

Big Red Fire Truck by Ken Wilson-Max

Curious George Visits the Fire Station by Margaret Rey

Fire Diary by Lily Rosenblatt

Fire Engine Freddy to the Rescue by Dawn Bentley

Fire Engines by Anne Rockwell

Fire! Fire! Said Mrs. McGuire by Bill Martin, Jr.

The Fire Station by Robert Munsch

The Fire Station (Who Works Here) by Lola Schaefer

Fire Truck by Peter Sis

Forgetful Little Fireman by Allan McDonald

I Want to Be a Firefighter by Stephanie Maze

Let's Visit the Fire Station by Marianne Johnston

Moonbear's Skyfire by Frank Asch

Smoky Night by Eve Bunting

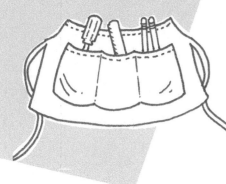

Fix-It Shop Prop Box

Vocabulary

adjust
alter
appliance
assemble
cog
computer chip
controls
damage
extension
gear
goggles
machine
measure
overhaul
parts
problem
pulley
recycle
remove
repair
replace
receipt
sand
spring
tool names (pliers,
    screwdriver, wrench, and
    so on)
wind
workbench

Basic Props

Appliance or owner's manuals
Broken toys
Carpenter's apron
Cash register or money drawer
Money, checkbook, credit card
Nuts, bolts, screws, washers,
    nails
Receipt book
Rubber bands
Ruler

Safety goggles
Small appliances (clock, lock,
    toaster, hair dryer, all with
    cords removed)
Tags or stickers
Tape
Tools (pliers, clamp, screw-
    driver, mallet, and others)
Wire

Additional Props

Clamps
Flashlight
Funnel
Measuring tape
Open/Closed sign
Paintbrush
Magnifying glass
Rags
Sandpaper
Scissors

Scraper
Styrofoam or rolled packing
    material
Twine
Tool box
Toothbrush
Tweezers
Wood scraps
Work gloves

Extension Activities

- Give children labeled photographs of tools to categorize.
- Provide simple objects that children can take apart and put back together.
- Sort nuts, bolts, screws, and nails into muffin tins.
- Demonstrate how to use a simple machine, such as an eggbeater. Ask children to describe how the machine works.
- Ask children to write or draw directions for fixing something.
- Design a new machine or robot. Construct it from nuts, bolts, wire, and recycled materials, such as boxes, paper tubes, egg cartons, foam pieces, spools, and plastic scraps.
- Hold pieces of sandpaper on a warming tray (lowest setting) while children draw on the sandpaper with crayons. Wax will melt, making a vivid picture.
- Give children different grades of sandpaper. Have them place drawing paper over the pieces of sandpaper and draw with crayons. Differences in texture will appear.

Related Literature

3 Pigs Garage by Peter Lippman
Call Mr. Vasquez, He'll Fix It! by Alice K. Flanagan
Edgar Badger's Fix-It Day by Monica Kulling
Fix-It by David McPhail
The Man Who Was Too Lazy to Fix Things by Phyllis Krasilovsky
Mum Can Fix It by Verna Allette Wilkins
Tool Book by Gail Gibbons

Flower Shop Prop Box

Vocabulary

arrangement
artificial
bloom
bud
clay
delivery
dozen
evergreen
florist
germinate
grower
harvest
leaf/stem/roots/bloom
life cycle
names of flowers
occasion
petal
pollen
price
purchase order
roots
stalk
stem
vase
weed

Basic Props

Artificial flowers
Blunt-edged scissors
Cash register or money drawer
Florist's clay
Money/checks/credit cards
Note cards/markers
Price tags
Ribbon
Sign with name of shop
Telephone
Vases (can be jars, clean milk cartons, and so on)

Additional Props

Baskets
Decorating materials (balloons, pipe cleaners, glitter, and so on)
Flower posters
Flower seeds
Gardening magazines
Greeting cards
Materials for children to create flowers (tissue paper, crepe paper, modeling clay, straws, tape, glue, and so on)
Materials to grow flowers from seed
Name tag/hat for delivery persons
Real flowers in season
Receipt pad

Extension Activities

- Brainstorm with children about occasions when flowers are used as a symbol of caring (sickness, death, birthdays, anniversaries, and so on)
- Visit a flower shop.
- Discuss the care of flowers.
- Teach the names of flower parts.
- Locate flower shop advertisements in the telephone book or newspaper.
- Create flowers from a variety of materials to sell in the shop.
- Provide wax paper and flowers or leaves. Under the supervision of an adult, children can press flowers between wax paper using a cool iron.

- Have a scavenger hunt to see how many things you can locate with flower names or that include flower parts such as soap, hand cream, and foods.
- Play a matching game using flower pictures and flower names.
- Buy an amaryllis bulb at the flower shop or supermarket, plant it, and chart its daily growth. Amaryllis grow an inch a day!

Related Literature

Alison's Zinnia by Anita Lobel
Chrysanthemum
    by Kevin Henkes
Dandelions by Eve Bunting
The Flower Alphabet Book
    by Jerry Pallotta
Flower Garden by Eve Bunting
The Legend of the Indian
    Paintbrush by Tomie dePaola
The Legend of the Poinsettia
    by Tomie dePaola
Ludlow Grows Up by Kelli C.
    Foster, et al
The Reason for a Flower
    by Ruth Heller
Red Leaf, Yellow Leaf
    by Lois Ehlert
Sunflower by Miela Ford
Tulips by Jay O'Callahan

Fruit and Vegetable Stand Prop Box

Vocabulary

berry
bunch
bush
care
crop
dozen
dried fruit
harvest
melon
nutritious
organic
peel
pit
pound
preserve
receipt
rind
ripe
root vegetable
salad
seasonal
stem
tree
variety
vine
weigh

Basic Props

Baskets for fruit and vegetables
Cash register or money box
Empty containers of jam, honey, raisins, fruits, and vegetables
Index cards and markers to make signs
Plastic fruit and vegetables
Play money, checks, credit cards
Price list
Receipt pad
Scale
Small paper bags
Strawberry baskets

Additional Props

Apron for checker
Assorted nuts
Dry-erase board and marker to list "specials"
Flyswatter
Non-perishable fruits and vegetables (gourds, Indian corn, dried beans, and so on)
Plastic bags
Signs (Fruits/Vegetables, Open/Closed, and so on)
Twisty ties

Extension Activities

- Provide a variety of fruit to be sold at the stand and then eaten for snack.
- Observe a stalk of celery in a glass of water with food coloring.
- Use fruit and vegetable seeds to make collages.
- Plant fruit and vegetable seeds in small pots. Put root vegetables, such as potatoes or carrots, in jars of water. Observe and record changes.
- Visit a produce stand or farmers' market.
- Draw the sequence of steps from seed to market.
- Identify the parts of a fruit or vegetable (leaves, seeds/pits, peel/rind).
- Serve raw vegetables with a dip for snack.
- Make a fruit salad for snack.
- Taste and compare fruits and vegetables in various forms (raw, cooked, in juice).
- Sort varieties of nuts and beans into categories. Graph the number of nuts in each category.
- Listen to Raffi's *Everything Grows* tape or CD.
- Using a balance scale, estimate and verify how many onions (for example) weigh the same as a cantaloupe.

- Provide children with a sheet on which to keep a weekly record of fruits and vegetables they eat each day.
- Draw a face on a small pumpkin or gourd and decorate with three-dimensional collage materials (buttons, yarn).
- Identify and compare different types of citrus fruits by size, shape, color, texture, and number of sections inside. Taste each and describe differences.

Related Literature

Eating the Alphabet
by Lois Ehlert
Farmer's Market
by Paul Brett Johnson
Fruits and Vegetables
by Lynda E. Chandler
The Giving Tree
by Shel Silverstein
How Do Apples Grow?
by Betsy Maestro
How Are You Peeling? by Saxton Freymann and Joost Elffers
Johnny Appleseed
by Patricia Demuth
Learning About Fruits
by Dot Barlowe
Learning About Vegetables
by Dot Barlowe
Oliver's Vegetables
by Vivian French
One Lonely Sea Horse by Saxton Freymann and Joost Elffers
The Story of Johnny Appleseed
by Aliki
The Tiny Seed by Eric Carle
Vegetable Garden
by Douglas Florian
When Vegetables Go Bad
by Don Gillmor and Marie-Louise Gay

Gardening Prop Box

Vocabulary

bitter
bloom
branch
bulb
compost
crop
fertilizer
flower names
fruit and vegetable names
germinate
harvest
hoe
insecticide
leaf
mulch
organic
pest
plant
pollinate
rake
roots
row
soil
sour
sow
spade
sprout
stem
sweet
till
trowel
weeds
worm

Basic Props

Artificial flowers, fruit, or
   vegetables stuck in
   inverted egg carton
   painted brown
Gardening gloves
Gardening tools
Hose length cut from
   old garden hose
Large piece of brown felt for "soil"
Neckerchief
Packages of seeds
Straw hat
Watering can

Additional Props

Baskets
Cups and soil to grow plants
Gardening magazines
Non-toxic empty garden product containers
Popsicle sticks and index cards to make plant labels
Seed catalogs
Small rake
Sunglasses
Vegetable/fruit/flower posters

Extension Activities

- Plant a small outdoor garden.
- Carve pumpkins and other vegetables.
- Make leaf rubbings with paper and the flat side of a crayon.
- Make a collage picture using different types of vegetable seeds.

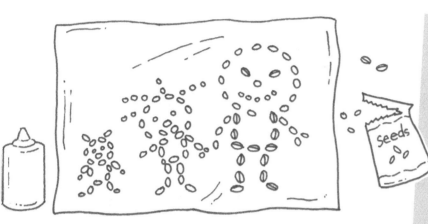

- Using pictures of different vegetables, create an imaginative vegetable person using vegetables as body parts.
- Using a small food scale and a variety of seeds, see how many seeds it takes for each variety to make an ounce. Graph the results.
- Add a few drops of food coloring to water in a glass. Stand a stalk of celery in the glass and watch what happens.
- Eat the edible parts of flowers for snack, such as sunflower seeds, stems (celery), and leaves (dandelion). Have potato chips, corn chips, popcorn, and other vegetable products and discuss their origins.
- Investigate the inside of a flower bulb using a magnifying glass.
- Look at different types of soil and sand and discuss what plants need to grow.
- Have a tasting party with a variety of exotic fruits and vegetables.
- Have a potato race. Use sticks to roll potatoes on the ground.
- Guess how many peas are in a pea pod, then break open the pod and count the peas. The peas can then be cooked for snack.
- Watch the video *The Magic School Bus Goes to Seed.*

Related Literature

Dancers in the Garden
   by Joanne Ryder
From Seed to Plant
   by Gail Gibbons
The Gardener by Sarah Stewart
A Gardener's Alphabet
   by Mary Azarian
The Garden of Happiness
   by Erika Tamar
Growing Vegetable Soup
   by Lois Ehlert
In My Garden: A Counting Book by Ward Schumaker
Jack's Garden by Henry Cole
Molly & Emmett's Surprise Garden by Marilyn Hafner
Patty's Pumpkin Patch
   by Teri Sloat
Planting a Rainbow
   by Lois Ehlert
Pumpkin Circle: The Story of a Garden by George Levenson
The Rose in My Garden
   by Arnold Lobel
The Surprise Garden
   by Zoe Hall
A Tree Is Nice
   by Janice May Udry

Gas Station/Garage Prop Box

Vocabulary

attendant
automobile
battery
brakes
fender
fuel
gallon
gasoline
headlights
hood
inspection
license plate
lubricate
maintenance
manager
mechanic
oil
pump
puncture
radiator
reliable
repair
service
station
tire
tool names
trunk
vehicle
windshield

Basic Props

Bucket
Cash register or money drawer
Clipboard and paper
Empty oil can or bottle
Hose length (for gas pump
    nozzle)
Flashlight
Funnel
Money, checks, credit card
Rags and sponges

Receipt book
Safety goggles
Shirts with car or gasoline
    brand patches sewn or
    drawn on
Spray bottle
Tire pump
Tools (pliers, screwdrivers,
    wrenches, and so on)

Additional Props

Auto parts (cleaned)
Automotive supply catalogues
Baseball caps
Car ads
Car service diagrams
Gas pump (labeled box with
    hose attached)
Keys
Maps
Paper towels

Rubber gloves
Rubber patches
Squeegee
Telephone
Tire gauge
Tire inner tubes
Tool catalogues
Wallet and purse
Wastebasket

Extension Activities

- Describe and demonstrate the different parts of your car (engine, fenders, gas tank, trunk, headlights). Then ask children to draw your car.
- Create a car from boxes and scrap materials.
- Visit a gas station.
- Invite a mechanic or gas station manager to visit.
- Wash and "service" the tricycles, bikes, and wagons on the playground.
- Put small amounts of paint in pie tins. Dip toy cars and trucks into paint and "drive" them across paper.
- Construct roads and buildings (including a service station) out of blocks.

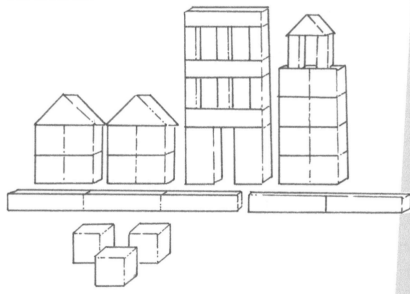

- Estimate how many cups make a gallon. Have children water cup by cup to determine the number.
- Take a walk in the school parking lot. Record particular numbers, letters, or letter combinations on car license plates.

Related Literature

Auto Mechanic
   by Douglas Florian
Cars by Anne F. Rockwell
Freddy Fixer Builds a Car
   by George Johansson and
   Jens Ahlbrom
Good Driving, Amelia Bedelia
   by Herman Parish
The Little Auto by Lois Lenski
Minton Goes Driving by Anna
   Fienberg and Kim Gamble
Miss Spider's New Car
   by David Kirk
Mr. Frumble's New Car
   by Richard Scarry
Mr. Yee Fixes Cars
   by Alice K. Flanagan
*Richard Scarry's Cars and
   Trucks and Things That Go*
   by Richard Scarry
Truck by Donald Crews
Trucks: Giants of the Highway
   by Ken Robbins
What Makes a Car Go?
   by Sophy Tahta

Hair Salon/Barber Shop Prop Box

Vocabulary

appearance
appointment
bald
bangs
beard
braids
curly
dye
fine
grooming
mustache
permanent
reflection
shampoo
shave
sideburns
straight
style
texture
thick
thin
trim
wave

Basic Props

Appointment book
Comb and brush
Clock
Curlers
Hair dryer (with cord removed)
Hairstyle album or magazines
Mirror
Plastic cape (made from large trash bag)
Plastic scissors (with aluminum blade removed)

Play money, checks, credit card
Price list
Safety razor with blade removed
Shampoo and conditioner bottles
Shaving cup and brush
Towels

Additional Props

Barber pole (paper towel roll covered with striped paper)
Barrettes and bobby pins
Empty containers of grooming products
Dishwashing tub
Electric shaver (with cord removed)
Hair ribbons
Headbands

Mannequin head
Open/Closed sign
Plastic glasses with mustache attached
Rubber gloves
Scrunchies
Telephone
Tip cup
Wigs

Extension Activities

- Group children by hair color or length of hair and graph results.
- "Shave" with shaving cream and craft sticks.
- With parents' permission, let children sculpt their hair (and yours!) with hair gel.
- Categorize magazine photos of people by hair color, style, and so on.
- Examine different strands of hair under a magnifying glass.
- Measure and record the length of children's hair.
- Visit a barbershop or unisex hair salon.
- Use scraps of fabric, fur, yarn, cotton balls, and sandpaper to make hair and beards on pictures.
- Tie three strands of thick yarn to a chair back and teach children how to braid.

Related Literature

Day of the Bad Haircut
  by Eva Moore
Don't Cut My Hair
  by Hans Wilhelm
Happy to Be Nappy
  by bell hooks
*How Emily Blair Got Her
  Fabulous Hair* by Susan
  Garrison Beroza
I Love My Hair
  by Natasha Tarpley
Mop Top by Don Freeman
Nappy Hair
  by Carolivia Herron
Saturday at the New You
  by Barbara E. Barber
Stephanie's Ponytail
  by Robert Munsch
Uncle Jed's Barbershop
  by James Ransome and
  Margaree King Mitchell

Health Club Prop Box

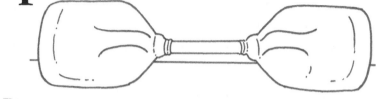

Vocabulary

aerobic
athletic
balance
barbells
endurance
exercise
fitness
flexible
gymnastics
healthy
heart rate
in shape
jogging
joint
muscle
perspiration
pulse
push up
repetition
skip
stretch
train
trampoline
weight
workout
yoga

Basic Props

Athletic shoes
Barbells (dowel with gallon milk jugs on both ends)
Exercise equipment
Gym bags
Height chart
Mirror
Scale
Shorts
Sweat bands
Tank tops
Water bottles

Additional Props

Exercise chart with dates and children's names
Exercise mats
Fitness magazines
Small boxes for step aerobics
Small weights (made from large tinker toys)
Stopwatch or timer
Tape recorder and jazzy tape
Telephone
Towels

Extension Activities

- Space permitting, add a mini-trampoline, basketball hoop, low balance beam, and tumbling mat to the dramatic play center.
- Teach basic exercises (jumping jacks, modified push-ups, arm circles, and so on).
- Chart children's weights and heights.
- Invite a gym teacher, fitness expert, or medical professional to talk about the importance of exercising.
- Hold an "Olympics" on the playground with areas for running relays, gymnastics, jumping, an obstacle course, and a beanbag toss.
- Help children find the large muscles in their bodies using a demonstration chart.
- Create individual charts to record the numbers of exercise movements children can do or the time it takes them to run a certain distance. Emphasize self-improvement rather than competition.
- Teach children to find their pulses. Have them check their pulses before and after exercising.

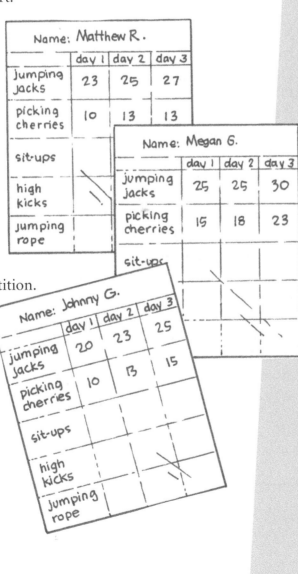

Related Literature

Angelina and Alice
  by Katharine Holabird
Billy the Great by Rosa Guy
Get Moving: Tips on Exercise
  by Kathy Feeney
Leon and Albertine
  by Christine Davenier
Little Miss Somersault
  by Roger Hargreaves
Mr. Strong by Roger Hargreaves
My Feet by Aliki
Norma Jean, Jumping Bean
  by Joanna Cole
The Tightrope Walker
  by Bernadette Gervais and
  Francisco Pittau
*A Yoga Parade of Animals: A
  First Picture Book of Yoga for
  Children* by Pauline Mainland

Ice Cream Shop Prop Box

Vocabulary

banana split
cherry
cone
counter
dairy
flavors (names of flavors)
freezer
frozen yogurt
gallon
ice cream sundae
milk shake
pint
quart
scoop
serve
sherbet
sorbet
syrup
topping
whipped cream

Basic Props

Cash register or money drawer
Empty plastic ice cream containers (ask ice cream shops)
Hats for clerks
Ice cream scoop
Ice cream shop posters with pictures of ice cream cones, sundaes, and so on
Money/checks/credit cards
Paper cups
Plastic bowls
Plastic spoons
Price list
Sign with name of shop

Additional Props

Artificial bananas cut in half lengthwise
Blender (with blade and cord removed)
Ice cream "toppings" made from paper confetti
Labels for ice cream containers
Paper cones made from brown paper
Paper napkins
Spray paint Ping-Pong balls for ice cream or make pompom balls from yarn (See directions in Appendix, page 126.)
Straws, empty soda bottles
Water pitcher

Extension Activities

- Make ice cream with an electric ice cream maker and "sell" it for snack in the ice cream shop.
- Discuss the origins of ingredients in ice cream (milk, sugar, and other ingredients).
- Using a felt board and three different felt ice cream scoop flavors, determine how many different combinations of ice cream cones can be made from these three scoops.
- Have an ice cream taste-testing party. Graph each child's ice cream preference.
- Using a variety of ice cream container sizes, guess and check how many Ping-Pong ball "scoops" will fit in each one.

- Create a new flavor of ice cream and describe the ingredients. Advertise it in the ice cream shop.
- Visit an ice cream factory to see how ice cream is made and packaged.
- Use brand-name ice cream containers and alphabetize the names.
- Make up a song such as "Do You Know the Ice Cream Man?" to the tune of "Do You Know the Muffin Man?"

Related Literature

Alligator Ice Cream
  by Cherene Raphael
Curious George Goes to an Ice Cream Shop by Margaret and H. A. Rey
From Cow to Ice Cream
  by Bertram T. Knight
I Like Ice Cream
  by Robin Pickering
Ice Cream at the Castle
  by Ann Love
Ice Cream Dream
  by Dave Goodale
Ice Cream Fun Day
  by Kitty Richards
The Ice Cream King
  by Greg McEvy
Ice Cream Larry
  by Daniel Manus Pinkwater
Ice Cream, the Whole Scoop
  by Gail Damerow
Isaac the Ice Cream Truck
  by Scott Santow
Let's Find Out About Ice Cream
  by Mary Ebeltoft Reid
Pistachio Peak: An Ice Cream Fairy Tale That Will Melt Your Heart by Noreen Wise
Shiny Ice Cream Truck
  by Jennifer Frantz
Simply Delicious
  by Margaret Mahy

Library Prop Box

Vocabulary

alphabetical order
author
biography
Bookmobile
borrow
Braille
Caldecott books
chapter
check-out
dictionary
due date
fact
fairy tale
fantasy
fiction
filing system
folk tale
history
illustrator
librarian
loan
Newberry books
nonfiction
novel
overdue
periodicals
poetry
reference
reserved
return
short story
title

Basic Props

Books
Calendar
Date stamp and ink pad
Index cards
Library cards
Magazines
Name tags (Librarian, Reference, Desk Clerk)
Newspapers
Pocket chart
Signs (Fiction, Nonfiction, Poetry, Information, Return Books
   Here, Quiet, and so on)
Stickers

Additional Props

Book display rack
Cash register or money box
Computer keyboard or typewriter
Eyeglasses without lenses
Index card file box
Pencil holder
Play money (to pay fines)
Posters of books
Small bulletin board
Telephone
Telephone book

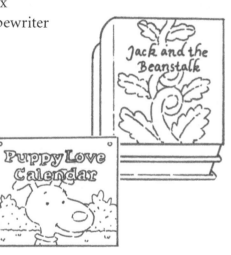

Extension Activities

- Make bookmarks.
- Sort books from the classroom library into categories (fiction, nonfiction, poetry, and so on). Arrange books alphabetically by author.
- Discuss parts of a book (cover, title page, table of contents, and so on).
- Visit the school library to check out a book. Review check-out procedures.
- Visit the local library during story hour.
- Bind children's drawings or stories together to make individual or class books. Exhibit in the classroom library.

- Send home application forms for city/county library cards. Follow up to make sure all children get a card.
- Design a book jacket for a favorite story.

Related Literature

Aunt Chip and the Great Triple Creek Dam Affair
  by Patricia Polacco
Check It Out!: The Book About Libraries by Gail Gibbons
Clara and the Bookwagon
  by Nancy Smiler Levinson
A Day With a Librarian
  by Jan Kottke
I Love Going Through This Book
  by Robert Burleigh
I Took My Frog to the Library
  by Eric A. Kimmel
The Library by Sarah Stewart
The Library Dragon
  by Carmen Agra Deedy
Library Lil by Suzanne Williams
Library: Who Works Here?
  by Lola M. Schaefer
Nicholas at the Library
  by Hazel Hutchins
Richard Wright and the Library Card by William Miller
Stella Louella's Runaway Book
  by Lisa Campbell Ernst
Tomas and the Library Lady
  by Pat Mora and Raul Colon

Magician Prop Box

Vocabulary

abracadabra
admission
appear
assistant
bouquet
club, diamond, heart,
   spade
disappear
illusion
imagine
magic
observe
pretend
shuffle
switch
top hat
trick
wand
wizard

Basic Props

Black or red material cut for a cape
Book of tricks for children to imitate
Bunch of artificial flowers
Deck of cards
Magician's hat (See directions in Appendix, page 125.)
Silk scarves
Small stuffed animal
Small table
Wand (made from a dowel painted black, with a silver tip painted
   on one end)

Additional Props

Blank notebook for children to record their own magic tricks
Bow tie
Cloth to cover table or hat
Clothing for assistant such as a large colorful shirt
Dice
Money
Sign for magician's name
Tickets to magic show
Watch
White gloves

Extension Activities

- Show children a few simple magic tricks.

- Put on a magic show.

- Watch a video of a real magician and see if children can figure out how the illusions are done.

- Explain that magic is done by fooling the eye and is not a special power, but only done for surprise and fun.

- Create a "magic" snack, turning powder and water into Jell-O!

- Use a quilter's marker that disappears within a few hours to write a disappearing message on a piece of cloth.

- Write on magic slates (found in variety stores).

- Experiment with sunprint paper outdoors (available at any scientific supply store). Follow directions on package.

- Do a white-on-white crayon rub. Draw a picture on white paper with a white crayon. Then brush the entire picture with one watercolor paint. Drawing will appear magically.

Related Literature

50 Nifty Super Magic Tricks by Shawn McMaster

Abracadabra and the Tooth Witch by Nurit Karlin

Abracadabra by Ingrid and Dieter Schubert

Harold and Chester in Rabbit-Cadabra by James Howe

Jasper & the Mixed-Up Dragon by Tracey West

Meredith's Mixed-Up Magic by Dorothea Lachner

Mixed-Up Magic by Gail Herman

Molly's Magic Carpet by Emma Fischel

The Sorcerer's Apprentice by Carla Jablonski

Sylvester and the Magic Pebble by William Steig

The Wizard, the Fairy, and the Magic Chicken by Helen Lester

Movie Theater Prop Box

Vocabulary

action
actor
actress
admission
adventure
animation
advertisement
camera
cartoon
comedy
concession
credits
critic
director
documentary
entrance
exit
feature
film
marquee
matinee
preview
producer
projector
rating
reel
refreshments
stub
ticket
usher
whisper

Basic Props

Candy boxes
Cash register or money box
Jackets for ticket-seller and
  ticket-taker
Plastic/paper cups
Play money, checks, credit cards
Popcorn boxes (cotton balls or
  packing peanuts can be used
  for popcorn)

Signs (Coming Attractions,
  Open/Closed, Sold Out,
  Concessions, and so on)
Tickets
White sheet or window shade
  for screen

Additional Props

Assorted clothing for actors
  and actresses
Bow tie and cummerbund
  for usher
Movie posters

Projector (shoebox with hinged
  lid, paper tube lens, and
  paper plate film reels)
Ticket booth (large box)
Wallets and purses

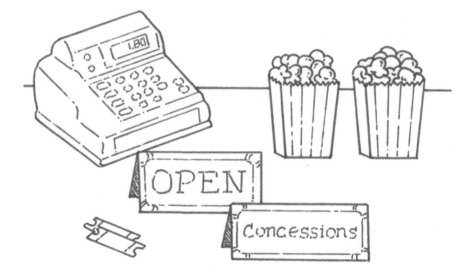

Extension Activities

- Divide children into actors and audience. Shine a light onto a sheet. Put the actors in the area between the light and the sheet. Their shadows will be projected on the sheet for viewing by the audience seated on the other side of the sheet.

- Write titles for their movies on sentence strips.
- Provide poster-sized paper for children to create advertisements for their favorite movies.
- Make popcorn. Measure the amount of unpopped kernels and compare to the amount of popped corn.
- Using a microphone (paper roll with Ping-Pong ball on end), invite children to interview each other about their favorite movies.
- Provide newspapers and a list of children's movies. Have children locate and circle the movies.

Related Literature

Angelina on Stage
  by Katharine Holabird
At the Movie Theater
  by Sandy Francis
The Berenstain Bears Get Stage Fright by Stan and Jan Berenstain
The Bionic Bunny Show
  by Marc Brown and Laurene Krasny Brown
Curious George Goes to a Movie
  by Margaret and H.A. Rey
On Stage and Backstage
  by Ann Hayes
The Saturday Kid
  by Cheryl Carlesimo
Shadows by Carolyn B. Otto

Optometrist Prop Box

Vocabulary

adjust
blink
blurry
bridge
bright
clear
contact lenses
correction
dim
distant/far
eyebrows
eye chart
eyelashes
eyelids
eyesight
farsighted
frame
glasses
hinge
iris
lens
magnify
near/close
nearsighted
prescription
pupils
receptionist
sensitive
squint
stem
vision
wink

Basic Props

Black cardboard for eye cover
Cash register or money drawer
Children's inexpensive sunglasses
Eye chart (with letters or pictures)
Mirror
Money/credit cards/checks
Name tag for optometrist
Old glasses with lenses removed
Prescription pad
Sign for shop
White shirt for lab coat

Additional Props

Binoculars or Viewmaster (to simulate viewing machine)
Empty contact lens bottles
Empty contact lens boxes (eye drops, cleaner)
Pictures/posters of people wearing glasses
Price chart
Small flashlight
Small magnifying glass
Squares of soft cloth to clean glasses
Thin, clear plastic cut into contact lens and eyeglass shapes
Used eyeglasses cases

Extension Activities

- Create an eye chart using rubber stamps and ink pad.
- Discuss the reasons people need to get their eyes checked.
- Do a self-portrait wearing glasses.
- Visit an optometrist's office to see the real equipment.
- Count how many people you see in one day who wear glasses.
- Cover empty eyeglass frames with colored plastic wrap and have children wear them to see how the world looks different through colored lenses. Have a blue day, a red day, and so on.
- Rent a 3-D children's movie along with 3-D glasses for everyone.
- Using a model of an eye, explain how the eye works like a camera.
- Using old frames and a variety of creative materials, have a decorating contest to see who can come up with the most creative, outlandish pair of glasses.
- Create eyeglasses using pipe cleaners, or binoculars from paper tubes.
- Play the game "I Spy" ("I spy someone with red shoes").
- Chart the color of each child's eyes.

Related Literature

All the Better to See You With
   by Margret Wild
Arthur's Eyes by Marc Brown
*Baby Duck and the Bad
   Eyeglasses* by Amy Hest
Blueberry Eyes
   by Monica Driscoll Beatty
Chimps Don't Wear Glasses
   by Laura Numeroff
Chuckie Visits the Eye Doctor
   by Luke David
Glasses: Who Needs 'Em?
   by Lane Smith
*Luna & the Big Blur: A Story for
   Children Who Wear Glasses*
   by Shirley Day
The Magic Spectacles
   by Gordon Rowe

Paint Store Prop Box

Vocabulary

border
bright
bristles
canvas
color names
cover
dark
decorate
design
detail
edge
foam
fumes
gallon
light
mix
mural
pale
paste
preparation
primary colors
protect
quart
roller
rough
secondary colors
smooth
spectrum
sponge
texture
tint

Basic Props

Cash register or money box
Color samples or color charts
Drop cloth
Mixing bucket
Paint cans
Paint roller
Paint stirrers
Paint tray
Paintbrushes

Plastic gloves
Play money, checks, credit cards
Rags
Receipt pad
Sandpaper
Sponges
Wallpaper sample book
Wet Paint signs

Additional Props

Color paddles
Dust masks
Home decorating magazines
Items made out of wood to "paint"
Masking tape
Paint can opener

Paint wand
Paint pad
Safety goggles
Scissors
White shirts and pants

Extension Activities

- Visit a local paint or hardware store.
- Let children paint playground equipment, building walls, or sidewalk with water.
- Use butcher paper to paint a group mural on the cement or attach paper to a fence.
- Provide primary colors of tempera paint for easel painting.
- Place red, yellow, and blue food coloring mixed with a little water in small bowls. Use eyedroppers to drop colored water onto paper towels to see how colors mix.
- Sort paint samples into the seven colors of the rainbow (red, orange, yellow, green, blue, indigo, and violet).
- Match decorator paint samples by mixing small amounts of tempera or watercolor paint in Styrofoam egg cartons.
- Add paint samples and wallpaper scraps to the art center so children can draw and decorate their favorite room.
- Cut up paint sample strips. Have children sequence the color hues from light to dark.
- Graph each child's favorite colors.

Favorite Colors

Red	Yellow	Blue	Green	Purple	Orange
Sally	Chris	Jose	Anna	Sarah	Peter
Sam		Mike		Cindy	
Li					
Kate					

Related Literature

The Art Lesson
  by Tomie dePaola
Color Dance by Ann Jonas
The Magic Paintbrush
  by Robin Muller
Matthew's Dream
  by Leo Lionni
The Mixed-Up Chameleon
  by Eric Carle
My Crayons Talk
  by Patricia Hubbard
The Painter
  by Peter Catalanotto
*The Painter Who Loved
  Chickens* by Olivier Dunrea
Planting a Rainbow
  by Lois Ehlert
*The Wilsons, A House-Painting
  Team* by Alice K. Flanagan

Pet Shop Prop Box

Vocabulary

amphibian
bark
cat
chirp
collar
companionship
dog
furry
gerbil
goldfish
groom
healthy
howl
leash
license
lizard
meow
parrot
parts of animals (beak, paws, scales, gills, and so on)
pet
purchase
reptile
responsibility
sale
screech
snake
soft

Basic Props

Cash register or money drawer
Empty boxes of pet food
Fish tank or plastic fish bowl/fish net/goldfish snack cookies
Leashes, collars, tags
Materials to make sale signs
Money/checks/credit cards
Name tags for clerks
Price list
Sign with store name
Variety of stuffed or plastic toys representing mammals, birds, reptiles, fish, and amphibians

Additional Props

Bird cage
Broom (to clean shop)
Cages for pets made from boxes or laundry baskets
Pet care pamphlets (acquired from veterinarian)
Pet licenses
Pet toys
Pictures of children's pets
Posters from real pet shop
Supplies for pet grooming (combs, brushes, empty shampoo bottles, toothbrush, toothpaste tube, and so on)
Water dishes made from margarine tins

Extension Activities

- Use poster paper and markers to create advertisements for the pet shop.
- Have children fish for their snack using goldfish snack crackers, a large bowl, and a fishnet. Bake cookies in the shape of dog biscuits.
- Provide clay and feathers and have children create birds to be sold in the pet shop.

- Brainstorm a price list for pets and display it in the play center.
- Invite a groomer to demonstrate pet grooming.
- Discuss the responsibilities of pet ownership.
- Gather pictures of different kinds of animals and sort into two categories: good for a pet and not good for a pet; with or without tails; four-footed and two-footed; and so on.
- Cut out pictures of animals and then cut them apart. Mix and match parts to create a new pet. Name the pet.
- Invite a person with a visual or hearing impairment and his or her trained dog to visit the children and explain the special training and help the animal provides.
- Visit a local pet shop or Humane Society.

Related Literature

Arthur's Pet Business
   by Marc Tolon Brown
Barney Goes to the Pet Shop
   by Mark Bernthal
Big Pets by Lane Smith
Fish (All About Pets) by Helen
   Frost and Gail Saunders-Smith
Helen the Fish by Virginia Kroll
How Smudge Came
   by Nan Gregory
I Need a Snake by Lynne Jonell
Mama Cat Has 3 Kittens
   by Denise Fleming
My Big Dog
   by Susan Steven Crummel
My Cats Nick & Nora
   by Isabelle Harper
My Dog Rosie
   by Isabelle Harper
Pet Shop by Frank Endersby
The Pet Shop Mouse
   by Judy Schrecker
Pet Show by Ezra Jack Keats
Queenie, One of the Family
   by Bob Graham

Picnic Prop Box

Vocabulary

ants
appetite
barbecue
checkered
container
grill
holiday
outdoors
outing
park
picnic
recreation
relaxation
shade
spices
sunburn
suntan
utensils

Basic Props

Artificial food
Balls
Baseball hats
Blanket to sit on
Books or magazines to read
Empty soda bottles
Paper or cloth napkins
Paper or plastic plates, cups
Picnic basket
Plastic utensils
Storage containers
Sunglasses

Additional Props

Artificial fish (for pond, with magnets attached to fish)
Artificial flowers
Board game such as checkers
Bubble wand and bubble soap
Butterfly net/butterflies
Camera
Empty suntan lotion tubes
Fishing pole with magnet on end of string
Jump rope
Ketchup/mustard bottles
Large piece of blue material for pond
Large piece of green material for grass
Plastic ants
Radio
Tablecloth

Extension Activities

- Mold food from playdough.
- Investigate different types of butterflies.
- Create a favorite picnic meal menu.
- Ask children to bring in family pictures of picnics and create a class book.

- Show children how to play games such as jacks, jump rope, and tag.
- Have a lunchtime picnic with the whole group.
- Discuss outdoor safety (prevention of sunburn, water safety, and so on).
- Teach games children can play at a picnic, such as tag and baseball.
- Make checkered placemats for a picnic by weaving red and white paper strips.

Related Literature

Halmoni and the Picnic
  by Sook Nyul Choi
One Hundred Hungry Ants
  by Elinor Pinczes
Packing for a Picnic by Lorraine
  Long and Mary Low
The Picnic by Ruth Brown
Picnic at Jigsaw Farm
  by Jennie Maizels
Picnic at Mudsock Meadow
  by Patricia Polacco
Picnic Farm
  by Christine Morton
A Picnic in October
  by Eve Bunting
Pig Picnic by Patricia Hubbell
The Pig's Picnic by Keiko Kasza
The Rattlebang Picnic
  by Margaret Mahy
The School Picnic by Jan Steffy
The Surprise Picnic
  by John S. Goodall
The Teddy Bears' Picnic
  by Jimmy Kennedy
*We Had a Picnic This Sunday
  Past* by Jacqueline Woodson

Pioneers Prop Box

Vocabulary

blacksmith
cabin
calico
caravan
chuck wagon
covered wagon
desert
diary
fort
frontier
gold rush
harness
herd
horse
horseback
plains
lantern
mining
mule
Native American
nugget
ore
ox cart
Pony Express
reins
scout
settlers
survival
territory
trading post
trail boss
trapper
tribe
wagon train
wilderness
wrangler

Basic Props

Bandanas
Bed roll (blanket or quilt tied with string or rope)
Bonnets
Campfire (scrap wood with crepe paper flames)
Cooking pot
Cowboy boots
Cowboy hats
Dishes, utensils (preferably metal)
Doll and baby blankets
Gold nuggets (rocks painted gold)
Letter-writing materials
Long skirts
Pie pan (for panning for gold)
Work gloves

Additional Props

Burlap bags
Carpet beater
Cornhusk dolls (made from tamale wrappers)
Clothesline (to hang rug over)
Flannel shirt
Lantern
Rocking horses, saw horses, or stick horses
Rug
Shawl

Extension Activities

- Tape flexible tent tubes on top of a table and cover with a white sheet to make a covered wagon. Place sawhorses with reins in front of it. Make a smaller covered wagon by securing half of a hula hoop to a child's wagon. Cover with sheet remnant.

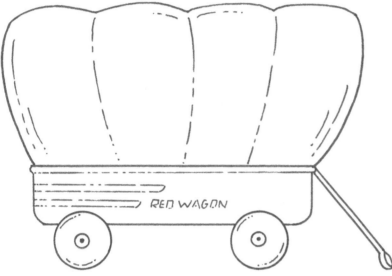

RED WAGON

- Drape a small rug or blanket over a clothesline to strike with a carpet beater.
- Reenact one of the stories listed to the right.
- Use cornhusks, sticks, strips of leather, and twine to create toys.
- Write a letter to a friend about traveling or living on the frontier.
- Pan for gold on the playground. Put sand, gold nuggets (small rocks spray painted gold), and water in a tub. Use pie tins with holes to find gold.
- Make handkerchief dolls out of small Styrofoam or Ping-Pong balls covered with a handkerchief and tied with string. Draw faces on the ball section with markers.
- Out on the playground, create a relief map of the terrain traveled by pioneers. Geographic features can include plains, mountains, valleys, and forests.
- Teach children songs and games played by pioneer children.
- Provide materials to build pioneer homes (log cabin, sod house, dugout).

Related Literature

Aunt Clara Brown: Official Pioneer by Linda Lowery
Dakota Dugout by Ann Warren Turner
Gold Fever! Tales from the California Gold Rush edited by Rosalyn Schanzer
Johnny Appleseed by Rosemary and Stephen Vincent Benet
If You Traveled West in a Covered Wagon by Ellen Levine
I Have Heard of a Land by Joyce Carol Thomas
The Ox Cart Man by Donald Hall
Prairie Dog Pioneers by Craig Spearing Harper
Sod House on the Great Plains by Glen Rounds
Striking It Rich: The Story of the California Gold Rush by Stephen Krensky
The Wagon Train (Life in the Old West) by Bobbie Kalman
Westward Ho!: The Story of the Pioneers by Lucille Recht Penner
The Zebra-Riding Cowboy: A Folk Song From the Old West by Angela Shelf Medearis

Post Office Prop Box

Vocabulary

address
advertisement
air mail
cancel
collection
correspondence
delivery
envelope
express mail
forward
insurance
invitation
letter
letter carrier
mail bag
mailbox
names of city, state, and
  country
official
pen pal
P. O. Box
postage
postal rate chart
postal worker
postcard
rate
receipt
return address
scale
sender
zip code

Basic Props

Badges
Blue shirts
Envelopes
Hat
Ink pad and stamps
Mailbag
Money
Pencils/markers

Postal rate chart
Postcards
Scale
Sheets of address labels that can
  be cut to create stamps
Stickers as stamp substitutes
Teacher-made mailbox
Writing paper

Additional Props

Address forwarding cards
Alphabetized name cards in
  box
Boxes, wrapping paper, tape,
  string for mailing
Calculator
Canceled stamps with glue stick
Child-size mail uniform
  (acquired from Post Office)
Express mail envelopes

Labels
Mailing forms
Picture atlas
Post Office coloring book
Postal rate chart
Real stamps to buy
Stamp posters
Telephone
Telephone book

Extension Activities

- Visit the local Post Office, Federal Express, or UPS plants.
- Read *The Jolly Postman* and give children postcards they can use to write to a fairy tale character.
- Find a pen pal in the same city or a different state.
- Start a group stamp collection.
- Set up a writing center with a variety of materials to encourage writing. Children can create their own stationery from supplied art materials.
- Provide a variety of different weight packages and a scale. Weigh and chart results.

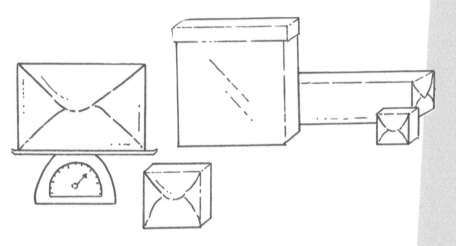

- Make a shoebox mailbox with a numerical address for each child. Have a rotating schedule for children to take turns delivering mail to their friends.
- Make cards with children's names and photos. Alphabetize the cards.
- Have each child find his or her family in the telephone book.
- Set up a post office where children can buy real stamps and mail letters.
- If you live by the sea, send a note in a bottle.
- Cut fruit roll-ups into squares for stamps. Place these "stamps" on a graham cracker, and use cake decorating tubes to write addresses. Makes a great snack!
- Create a stamp to use in the Post Office play center.

Related Literature

A Letter to Amy
  by Ezra Jack Keats
Arthur's Pen Pal
  by Lillian Hoban
Dear Annie by Judith Caseley
Dear Daddy by John Schindel
Dear Mr. Blueberry
  by Simon James
Don't Forget to Write
  by Martina Selway
Love, Your Bear Pete
  by Dyan Sheldon
The Jolly Postman
  by Janet and Allan Ahlberg
Mailing May
  by Michael Tunnell
The Mysterious Penpal
  by Eli A. Cantillon
Never Mail an Elephant
  by Mike Thaler
No Mail for Mitchell
  by Catherine Siracusa
Pony Express by Steven Kroll
We Are Best Friends by Aliki
What the Mailman Brought
  by Carolyn Craven

Restaurant Prop Box

Vocabulary

bake
boil
broil
cafeteria
chef
customer
fast food
food names
fry
host/hostess
ingredients
menu
order
pan
portion
pot
recipe
reservation
roast
server
specials
spice names
steam
stove
thermometer
tip
utensils

Basic Props

Bowls
Chef's hat
Cooking utensils
Cups, plates, utensils
Empty spice jars
Fake food
Measuring cups/spoons
Menus

Money/checks/credit cards
Napkins
Pads/pencils for servers
Placemats or tablecloth
Potholders
Pots and pans
Salt and pepper shakers

Additional Props

Aprons
Artificial flowers for tables
Baking pans
Cash register or money drawer
Chalkboard to list daily specials
Chopsticks
Cook book
"Doggy bag" containers
Ketchup/mustard bottles
Meat thermometer

Music tapes and tape recorder
Playdough
Recipe box
Restaurant uniforms
Stove and refrigerator created
    from large boxes
Tablecloths
Telephone

Extension Activities

- Watch a cooking show on TV.
- Invite cafeteria chefs to do a cooking demonstration.
- Tour the school cafeteria kitchen.
- Choose the menu items for the restaurant from among family recipes.
- Prepare snack foods to be sold in the restaurant.
- Weave or decorate placemats.
- Make a graph of the children's favorite foods.
- Name the restaurant and create the sign.
- Demonstrate and have children practice how to set a table.
- Seriate different size plates and cups from smallest to largest.

- Count the number of items on real menus.
- Create foods for the restaurant from clay.
- Discuss the importance of storing foods properly to maintain freshness.

Related Literature

The Berenstain Bears Go Out to Eat by Stan Berenstain
Curious George and the Pizza by H. A. Rey
Dinner at the Panda Palace by Stephanie Calmenson
Friday Night at Hodges' Café by Tim Egan
Frog Goes to Dinner by Mercer Mayer
Froggy Eats Out by Jonathan London
Little Nino's Pizzeria by Karen Barbour
Pigs Will Be Pigs by Amy Axelrod
Sheep Out to Eat by Nancy Shaw
Teddy Bears Eat Out by Suzanne Gretz and Alison Sage
Toad Eats Out by Susan Schade

Safari Prop Box

Vocabulary

Africa
backpack
binoculars
camouflage
canteen
extinct
herd
jeep
jungle
lantern
names of birds
names of jungle animals
pith helmet
plain (savannah)
safari
snag
spotted
stalk
striped
watering hole

Basic Props

Animal ears and noses
Animal identification book
Animal masks
Animal tails
Binoculars
Bird masks
Canteen
Compass
Duffel bags
Flashlight
Maps
Safari hat
Safari vest
Stuffed jungle animals and
  birds
Sunglasses

Additional Props

Animal print fabrics
Animal puppets
Artificial plants
Backpack
Blue cloth to spread on the
  floor as a watering hole
Boots
Butterfly net
Empty sunscreen tubes
Fake logs for fire
Jungle print shirts
Lantern
Magnifying glass
Maps
Pith helmet
Safari travel brochures
Steering wheel for jeep
Tapes of jungle animal/birds
  sounds
Tents

Extension Activities

- Invite a guest speaker to come and share slides of a safari.
- Take a field trip to the zoo to study jungle animals.
- Watch a video about jungle animals (*National Geographic* has a big selection).
- Provide materials to create animal masks.
- Have children move like animals in the jungle as they listen to music.
- Match jungle animal babies with animal parents.
- Create maps to follow for a safari.
- Have children use clay to create jungle birds to hang in the room.
- Listen to a tape of jungle animal sounds and pick an animal card to match the sound.
- Use a globe to show the children where Africa is located and where safaris take place.

Related Literature

Animalia by Graeme Base
Baboon by Kate Banks
The Happy Hippopotami by Bill Martin Jr.
I'm Not Sleepy by Denys Cazet
Is Your Mama a Llama? by Deborah Guarino
Jungle Jack Hanna's Safari Adventure by Jack Hanna
Lazy Lion by Mwenye Hadithi
The Lion's Whiskers: An Ethiopian Folktale by Nancy Raines Day
Little Gorilla by Ruth Bornstein
One Day in the Jungle by Colin West
One Gorilla: A Counting Book by Atsuko Morozumi
Rumble in the Jungle by Giles Andreae
Where the Wild Things Are by Maurice Sendak
Why the Leopard Has Spots by Katherine Mead

Science Laboratory Prop Box

Vocabulary

accuracy
cause
compare
contamination
control
conclusion
effect
filter
discovery
disease
dissolve
expect
experiment
hypothesis
laboratory
measure
method
microscope
observe
predict
probability
procedure
protection
record
research
results
scientific
solution
theory
thermometer
test

Basic Props

Aluminum pie pans
Assorted items to "test," such as dirt, rocks, playdough, plant parts, cornmeal
Cotton swabs
Eyedroppers
Lab coats (white shirts)
Lab journal
Magnifying glass

Masks
Plastic gloves
Safety goggles
Spoons
Styrofoam egg cartons
Timer
Tongs
Tweezers

Additional Props

Coffee filters
Food coloring
Funnel
Litmus paper
Microscope
Petri dishes
Pipettes

Plexiglas microscope slides
Scale
Test tubes
Test tube holder
Thermometer
Transparency film
Tubing

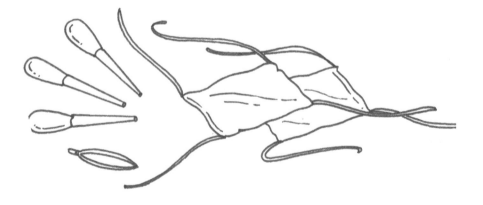

Extension Activities

- Have children look at onion skin, hair, bread mold, and a dead insect under a microscope and draw what they see.
- Demonstrate and discuss various states of water (solid, liquid, and gas).
- Observe the results of mixing different substances into water (for example, salt, powdered drink mix, sand, tea leaves, oil).

- Make "oobleck"—cornstarch mixed with colored water. (See recipe on page 129 of the Appendix.) Explore the oobleck using some of the science props listed on the previous page. Explore other substances, such as florist's clay, mud, or colored water. Discuss similarities and differences.
- Record the changes that happen to a variety of foods (for example, chocolate, gum, an apple slice, milk, Jell-O) when they are heated and cooled.
- Drop water onto sand using an eyedropper held 12" above the sand. Observe how craters form. Repeat the process on the playground.
- Experiment with growing plants. Put small potted plants in different locations (light and dark) and vary the amounts of water and food. Record observations.
- Show children how to read litmus paper that has been dipped in vinegar and a baking soda and water solution. Combine the two liquids and retest with the litmus paper.

Related Literature

Bartholomew and the Oobleck by Dr. Seuss

The Berenstain Bears' Science Fair by Stan and Jan Berenstain

The Case of the Stinky Science Project by James Preller

Eeny Meeny Miney Mole by Jane Yolen

Everyone Is a Scientist by Lisa Trumbauer

Experiments in Science: How Does It Work? by David Glover

Jan's Big Bang by Monica Hughes

The Living Earth by Eleonore Schmid

The Magic School Bus Ups and Downs: A Book About Floating and Sinking by Jane B. Mason, et al

The Quicksand Book by Tomie dePaola

Solid, Liquid, or Gas by Sally Hewitt

Tomatoes from Mars by Arthur Yorinks

Why I Sneeze, Shiver, Hiccup, and Yawn by Melvin Berger

Zoom by Istvan Banyai

Shoe Store Prop Box

Vocabulary

ankle
calf
canvas
comfortable
cost
buckle
eyelet
fastener
fit
heel
lace
leather
length
measure
polish
purchase
return
sale
selection
service
shoeshine
size
snap
sole
strap
toe
tongue
traction
tread
Velcro
width

Basic Props

Assorted shoes (boots, Chinese slippers, dress shoes, moccasins, sport shoes, sandals, and so on)
Cash register or money box
Play money, checks, credit cards
Price tags
Receipts
Shoe horn
Shoelaces

Shoe size measurer (made from cardboard or a ski boot carrier)
Socks and stockings
Shoeboxes

Additional Props

Bags
Brush, rag, sponge for cleaning
Floor mirror
Footrest
Knee-highs in assorted skin tones
Polishing cloth and brush
Shoe catalogues
Signs (shoe store name, Open/Closed, Sale, and so on)
Special types of shoes (ballet slippers, tap shoes, hiking or ski boots, and so on)
Telephone
Water bottle with sponge-tip applicator ("Bingo bottle") to use as "shoe polish"
Wooden shoe forms

Extension Activities

- Discuss various types of shoes and their functions.
- Take a field trip to a shoe store and/or shoe repair shop or visit a shoe factory to watch how shoes are made.
- Draw the sequence of buying a pair of shoes.
- Take a walk in the neighborhood to count different kinds of shoes people are wearing.
- Graph children's shoe sizes.
- Categorize pictures of shoes by function, material, type of fastener, and so on.
- Use clay or playdough to create shoe sculptures.
- Use shoe catalogues or newspapers with shoe ads to make price tags for shoes.
- Show children pictures of shoes from the past. Discuss similarities and differences with today's shoes.
- Have a "crazy shoe day." Invite children to decorate and wear an old pair of shoes.

Related Literature

Albert's Old Shoes by Stephen and Mary Jane Muir

Boot Weather by Judith Vigna

The Growing-Up Feet by Beverly Cleary, et al

New Shoes for Silvia by Johanna Hurwitz

New Shoes, Red Shoes by Susan Rollings

Not So Fast Songololo by Niki Daly

A Pair of Red Sneakers by Lisa Lawston

Red Dancing Shoes by Denise Lewis Patrick

Red Rubber Boot Day by Mary Lyn Ray

The Red Shoes by Barbara Bazilian

Shoes, Shoes, Shoes by Ann Morris

Whose Shoe? by Margaret Miller

Whose Shoes? by Anna Grossnickle Hines

Whose Shoes? by Brian Wildsmith

Space Prop Box

control panel

Vocabulary

astronaut
atmosphere
blast-off
cockpit
collect
controls
countdown
crew
exploration
fuel
galaxy
gravity
Johnson Space Center
Kennedy Space Center
launch
meteor
Milky Way
mission
NASA
orbit
planet
rocket
sample
satellite
shuttle
solar system
space station
space walk
weightless

Basic Props

Air tanks (See directions in Appendix, page 120.)
Headsets
"Moon" rocks
Log book
Resealable sandwich bags
Space center control panel (See directions in Appendix, page 124.)
Space helmets (See directions in Appendix, page 127.)
Trowel or small shovel

Additional Props

Backpacks (for space packs)
Computer keyboard
Flashlight
Frozen food trays
Magnifying glass to examine moon rocks
Packages of freeze-dried foods (found at camping stores)
Plastic gloves
Plastic tubes or short lengths of dryer hose
Spacesuit smocks (made from mylar, space blanket, or metallic surgery blanket)
Sports bottles with drinking tubes
Tweezers or tongs
Walkie talkies

Extension Activities

- Take a field trip to a planetarium or a natural science museum.
- Visit the NASA website (www.NASA.gov). (NASA also offers excellent educational materials that are free of charge.)
- Let children jump on the "moon" (sheets sewn together and filled with foam scraps). (See directions in Appendix, page 124.)
- Paint a large box to represent a space ship or lunar rover.
- Use paper tubes to make rocket ships.
- Make robots using milk cartons as the base.
- Play "space" music.
- Introduce the concept that planets revolve around the sun and rotate on their axes by having children act as planets traveling around a light bulb or flashlight.
- Use ink pads and star stamps to create a Milky Way on large sheets of paper. Tape to the ceiling.
- Cover the windows with black or blue paper into which small holes have been punched in the form of constellations. Turn out the lights to see the stars twinkle.
- Create your own planetarium by pasting fluorescent stars onto the walls and ceiling of a closet or large appliance box.

Robot

Related Literature

Arty the Part-Time Astronaut
   by Eddie Carbin
Earthdance by Lynn Reiser
Exploring Space by Michael Lye
Floating Home by David Getz
Grandpa Takes Me to the Moon
   by Timothy R. Gaffney
Have Space Suit, Will Travel
   by Robert A. Heinlein
Here in Space
   by David Milgrim
I Want to Be an Astronaut
   by Byron Barton
Louis and the Night Sky
   by Nicola Morgan
*The Magic School Bus Lost in
   the Solar System*
   by Joanna B. Cole
Man on the Moon
   by Anastasia Suen
Moongame by Frank Asch
The Shine Around the Moon
   by Roshni Mangal

Supermarket Prop Box

Vocabulary

advertisement
aisle
bagger
bar code
cart
cashier
checkout
coupon
customer
dairy foods
delivery
dozen
food names
fresh
frozen foods
Have a nice day!
May I help you?
ounce
pound
price
produce
purchase
sale
scan
shelf
Thank you!
weigh

Basic Props

Artificial foods
Cash register or money drawer
Coupons
Empty food containers
Money/checks/credit cards
Notepad to write grocery list
Paper bags
Paper products to buy
Plastic baskets to carry purchases and hold materials for purchase

Additional Props

Additional supermarket goods (health products, laundry supplies, makeup, magazines, greeting cards, flowers, and so on)
Cake decorating supplies
Coupon flyers from local supermarket
Credit cards, checkbook
Deli hat and apron
Freezer box
Imitation scanning box
Microphone to make announcements
Plastic eggs and egg cartons
Purse or wallet
Roll of numbers for use in deli line
Scales to weigh food
Shopping cart
Signs (store hours, store name, Open/Closed, Sale, Reduced, and so on)
Stickers on which to write prices

Extension Activities

- Take a field trip to the local supermarket. Find and purchase ingredients for a simple recipe for the children to make.
- Provide a variety of picture cards with supermarket supplies and sort by general category.
- Draw and color displays for the store.
- Discuss how foods are transported to the supermarket.
- Discuss the different jobs in the supermarket and provide opportunities for children to rotate jobs while playing.
- Locate and discuss store ads. Have the children create a newspaper ad about their store.
- Create coupons for use in the store.
- Put objects in a grocery bag and ask children to guess what the objects are from the clues you provide.
- Draw a supermarket floor plan on a large sheet of paper. Have children cut and sort pictures of grocery items from magazines and glue them in the correct section of the floor plan.
- Play Supermarket Bingo. Use duplicate store advertisements to create the Bingo cards and the Bingo calling cards.
- Provide cupcakes for snack. Let children decorate and sell the cupcakes in the grocery store.

Related Literature

At the Supermarket
  by David Hautzig
Believing Sophie
  by Hazel Hutchins
Bread Is for Eating
  by David Gershator, et al
Bunny Cakes
  by Rosemary Wells
Don't Forget the Bacon
  by Pat Hutchins
Down the Road
  by Alice Schertle
Farmer's Market
  by Paul Brett Johnson
Let's Go to the Supermarket!
  by Lorraine Gallacher
My Gran by Debbie Boon
My Little Supermarket: Learn and Play As You Shop and Look by Caroline Repchuk
The Shopping Basket
  by J. Burningham
Something Good
  by Robert Munsch
The Supermarket
  by Gail Saunders-Smith
Supermarket by Kathleen Knell
Supermarket (Who Works Here)
  by Lola M. Schaefer

Travel Agency Prop Box

Vocabulary

booking
camping
cruise
departure/arrival
destination
east
flight plan
hotel
international
itinerary
luggage
motel
national
national park
north
overseas
passport
reservation
road map
schedule
sightsee
south
time zone
tourist
transportation
travel
vacation
visa
west

Basic Props

Maps (free at travel agencies)
Money/credit cards
Nametags for travel agents
Note pad/pencils
Sign with name of travel agency
Teacher-made passports (few sheets of paper and a cover folded in half and stapled)
Teacher-made airline/bus tickets
Telephone
Travel brochures

Additional Props

Backpack
Blank sticky labels to make travel stickers to put on suitcase
Camera
Computer
Luggage tags
Several clocks to show different time zones
Suitcase
Travel posters, books, and videos (acquired from travel agencies)
Variety of clothing for travel to different climates (hats, scarves, and mittens; bathing suits and shorts, and so on)

Extension Activities

• Watch the video *Winnie the Pooh's Grand Adventure.*

• Write an imaginary travel journal.

• Choose a destination on a globe and plan a trip. Discuss the type of clothing and the method of travel required for the trip.

• Using a large map of the United States, have children place a pin on places they have visited.

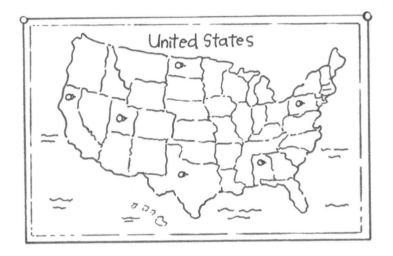

• Choose a travel destination and compare and contrast this place to the children's home city/state. Talk about foods, topography, climate, plants, housing, and so on.

• Discuss different modes of transportation with children and what is required for each one.

• Arrange chairs in a row and pretend to be on a plane or boat going on a vacation.

• Fill an empty suitcase with clothing appropriate for travel to either a warm or cold climate.

Related Literature

Amelia's Fantastic Flight
    by Rose Bursik
*As the Crow Flies, A First Book
    of Maps* by Gail Hartman
Clifford Takes a Trip
    by Norman Bridwell
Crazy for Canada
    by Noah Schwartz
Minnie and Moo Go to Paris
    by Denys Cazet
*Mr. Putter and Tabby Take the
    Train* by Cynthia Rylant
My Map Book by Sara Fanelli
My Mom Travels a Lot
    by Caroline Feller Bauer
*Stringbean's Trip to the Shining
    Sea* by Vera B. and Jennifer
    Williams
A Trip to the Ocean
    by John D. Morris
Vinnie in Egypt
    by Elizabeth Bott
Where Is Gah-Ning?
    by Robert Munsch

TV Production Studio Prop Box

Vocabulary

action
actor and actress
advertise
air
audience
broadcast
camera operator
channel
comedy
commercial
director
documentary
drama
episode
microphone
narrate
newscaster
product
production
program
reporter
screen
script
series
station
viewing

Basic Props

Camera
Clipboard and paper
Clock with posable hands
Clothing for actors and newscasters
Director's "take" prop (See directions in Appendix, page 122.)
Earphones/headset
Microphones (paper tube with styrofoam or Ping-Pong ball)
Mirror
Sunglasses
Telephone
TV guide

Additional Props

Clamp light
Dry-erase boards and markers
Make-up brushes
Movie camera (See directions in Appendix, page 126.)
Name cards for newscasters, director, and so on
Post-It notes
Products to advertise
Remote control device
Television made from cardboard box (with antennae)

Extension Activities

- Interview classmates for a news program.
- Create a television advertisement for a favorite book.
- Take a field trip to a television studio.
- Write a script for a television program.
- Videotape children as they demonstrate their talents, act out a story, or play a game. Ask them to narrate the tape as they watch it.
- Have children take turns videotaping a section of a "program."
- Make an advertisement for a type of supply or school product. Let them help videotape it.

Related Literature

The Bionic Bunny Show
  by Marc Tolon Brown
A Day in a Life of a TV
  Reporter by Linda Hayward
It's George by Miriam Cohen
Lights, Action, Land-Ho!
  by Judy Delton
Mouse TV by Matt Novak
Nibble, Nibble, Jenny Archer
  by Ellen Conford
Song and Dance Man
  by Karen Ackerman
Take a Look, It's in a Book: How
  Television Is Made at Reading
  Rainbow by Ronnie Krauss
TV Reporters by Tracey Boraas
Working at a TV Station
  by Gary Davis

Under the Sea Prop Box

Vocabulary

air tank
algae
anemone
coral
crab
depth
dive
dolphin
dune
eel
fins
flippers
gills
island
jellyfish
lobster
marine
migrate
ocean
octopus
oxygen
periscope
porthole
reef
salty

school (of fish)
sea life
seaweed
shark
shellfish
shipwreck
snorkel
squid
submarine
surface
tide
whale

Basic Props

Artificial plants
Beach towels
Blue, green, and purple streamers to hang from ceiling
Fish net
Flippers
Goggles
Ocean creatures to suspend from ceiling and put on floor
Old bathing suits
Seashells
Snorkel
Swim vest
Teacher-made fish fins

Additional Props

Air tanks (See directions in Appendix, page 120.)
Audiotapes of ocean sounds
Beach sand (spread over plastic on floor)
Field guide to sea life
Ocean posters
Octopus (See directions in Appendix, page 126.)
Painted T-shirts for fish bodies
Red oven mitts for lobster claws
Red vest for lobster
Scuba mask
Submarine (See directions in Appendix, page 128.)

Extension Activities

- Visit the local aquarium or invite an aquarium employee to speak to the class.
- Purchase sea monkeys at a pet store. Children can care for them and observe the changes.
- Use gummy fish for counting games.
- Using audiotapes, children can move to the sounds of the sea with scarves or streamers.
- Make edible aquariums by putting blue gelatin and gummy fish in clear plastic cups for a snack.
- Tack a fish net to the wall and weave ribbon through the net.
- Put a real aquarium together for the classroom. Let children select the fish.
- Put salt water in the water table and experiment with floating objects.
- Provide seashells for children to sort.
- Eat tuna on a half shell (clam or oyster shell).
- Using three large shells, play the shell game. Children guess which shell has an object under it.
- Find unusual ocean objects for display, such as a seahorse, starfish, conch shell, or sand dollar.

- Use a globe to show the migration of whales.
- Cut and paste duplicate pictures of fish on two sets of index cards and play "Go Fish."
- Have a crab race. Children lie on their backs, raise themselves up, and walk on their hands and feet.

Related Literature

Amos and Boris
  by William Steig
Commotion in the Ocean
  by Giles Andreae
Fish Eyes by Lois Ehlert
Fish Is Fish by Leo Lionni
*Is This a House for Hermit
  Crab?* by Megan McDonald
*The Magic School Bus on the
  Ocean Floor* by Joanna Cole
Ocean Alphabet Book
  by Jerry Pallotta
The Rainbow Fish
  by Marcus Pfister
Sea Animals by Pat L. Stewart
Sea Otter Inlet by Celia Godkin
Swimmy by Leo Leonni
The Whale's Song
  by Dyan Sheldon
What's in the Deep Blue Sea?
  by Peter Seymour

Veterinarian Prop Box

Vocabulary

beak
care
claw
collar
emergency
feathers
fever
first-aid
flea
fur
groom
heartworm
immunization
kennel
leash
license
paw
perch
prescription
responsibility
scales
stethoscope
surgery
temperature
tick
treat
vaccination
veterinarian
vitamins
whiskers
x-ray

Basic Props

Animal posters
Appointment pad
Bandages
Band-aids
Clipboard/paper
Cotton
Dry pet food
Empty pill bottles

Lab coat (white shirt)
Q-tips
Rubber gloves
Stethoscope
Stuffed animals
Telephone
Tongue depressors for splints

Additional Props

Animal care/health brochures
Birdcage
Blankets
Business cards
Cages made from overturned
    laundry baskets
Dog bones
Empty pet food cans
Leashes
Money/checks/credit cards
Old animal x-rays (obtained
    from veterinarian or made by
    drawing with marker on
    transparency sheets)

Pet carrying case
Pet collars
Pet food and water dishes
Pet toothbrush and toothpaste
Prescription pad
Small flashlight
Surgical mask
Thermometer
Weight scale

Extension Activities

- Have children bring in pictures of their pets to put in a class pet book.
- Discuss the responsibilities associated with having a pet.
- Take a field trip to a veterinarian's clinic.
- Adopt a small pet for the children to care for.
- Create a mural of pets and their habitats.
- Have a pet-naming contest for the class pet.
- Create a variety of pet songs to the tune of "I'm a Little Teapot."
- Invite children to move like their favorite pet and have the other children guess what they are.
- Invite a zookeeper to come in and explain how he or she helps to keep animal teeth healthy.

Related Literature

Barnyard Song
  by Rhonda Gowler Greene
Burt Dow, Deep Water Man
  by Robert McCloskey
Clifford the Small Red Puppy
  by Norman Bridwell
*Clifford El Pequeno Perro
  Colorado* by Norman
  Bridwell
I Want to Be a Veterinarian
  by Stephanie Maze and
  Catherine O'Neill Grace
The Little Puppy by Judy Dunn
My Dog Is Lost
  by Ezra Jack Keats
Patch the Perfect Kitten
  by Jenny Dale
Pet Show by Ezra Jack Keats
Pretzel by Margaret and
  H. A. Rey
The Puppy Who Wanted a Boy
  by Jane Thayer
*The Tenth Good Thing About
  Barney* by Judith Viorst
*The Tiger Has a Toothache:
  Helping Animals at the Zoo*
  by Patricia Lauber
Veterinarian
  by Kathleen Ermitage

Wash Day Prop Box

Vocabulary

button
collar
cotton
crease
cuff
denim
detergent
dryer
fabric
fold
fluff
hook
iron
ironing board
label
laundromat
laundry
nylon
press
sleeve
snap
soak
sort
stain
starch
stiff
suds
washer
wool
wring
zipper

Basic Props

Clothesline
Clothespins
Clothing to wash, including dolls' clothes
Drying rack
Empty detergent, bleach, and fabric softener containers
Hangers
Laundry baskets (labeled "dirty" and "clean," and so on)
Washboard
Washtub

Additional Props

Cloth diapers or small towels
Index cards or paper and markers for making labels
Iron (with cord removed)
Picture chart showing sequence of folding a diaper or towel into halves and quarters
Rubber gloves
Scrub brushes
Spray bottle
Washing machine and dryer (large boxes with cut-out doors and knobs/dials)

Extension Activities

- Sort clothing (dirty/clean, adult/children, whites/colors).
- Pair items that belong together (socks, short sets, and so on).
- Visit a laundromat.
- Fold diapers and towels.
- Add clothing, soap, and brushes to the water table.
- Sing "This Is the Way" (we wash our clothes, hang our clothes, fold our clothes, and so on).
- Use laundry soap to make a bubble solution and blow bubbles outside. (See recipe in Appendix, page 129.)
- Make a card game showing the steps to do laundry. Arrange the cards in the correct sequence.
- Stain pieces of cloth with grape juice. Put in different bowls containing different kinds of laundry detergents and let them soak for several hours. Ask children to predict which soap will clean the best. Check the results.

Related Literature

At the Laundromat
    by Christine Loomis
Aunt Lilly's Laundromat
    by Melanie Hope Greenberg
Dirty Laundry Pile: Poems in Different Voices by Paul Janeczko
The Great Soap-Bubble Ride
    by Susan Cornell Poskanzer
The Laundry Pile
    by Jeanne Face
The Low-Down Laundry Line Blues by C.M. Miller
Noddy's Wash Day Mix-Up
    by Gill Davies
A Pocket for Corduroy
    by Don Freeman
Wash Day by Charnan Simon
William Willya and the Washing Machine by Skip Masland

Wedding Prop Box

Vocabulary

aisle
anniversary
banquet
best man
bouquet
bride
bridesmaids
ceremony
father-in-law
guests
gown
groom
invitation
honeymoon
judge
mother-in-law
minister
organ
photographer
priest
promise
reception
usher
veil
vows

Basic Props

Artificial flowers
Cake (See directions in Appendix, page 122.)
Camera
Erasable invitations (laminated cards)
Fancy clothing for bride, groom, bridesmaids, ushers
   (representative of different cultures)
Guest book
Pictures of wedding ceremonies in various cultures
Veil (ruffled curtain or lacy fabric)

Additional Props

Black shirt or shawl for the minister/priest/rabbi
Bow-tie and cummerbund
Clothing for wedding guests
Flower basket
Jewelry
Marriage license
Menu for wedding reception
Pillow
Plates and utensils
Rings and ring boxes
Tablecloth
Tape of "Here Comes the Bride" or other suitable music
Travel brochures for honeymoon
Wedding magazines

Extension Activities

- Take photos of children staging weddings for a class wedding album.
- Invite parents from different cultures to show photos and tell about their cultures' wedding customs.
- Bake a wedding cake to celebrate the wedding of two stuffed animals. Hold the reception during snack.
- Ask parents to teach children some traditional dances done at weddings.
- Have children create invitations to the wedding of two stuffed animals.
- Glue photos of rings from a catalog onto index cards. Children can find pairs of rings or categorize them by type (for example: gold, silver, plain metal, with gems, and so on).
- Give children cut-out people shapes of various colors. They can use collage materials to make bride and groom paper dolls.

Related Literature

Helga's Dowry: A Troll Love Story by Tomie dePaola

Jumping the Broom by Courtni Crump Wright

The Keeping Quilt by Patricia Polacco

Mountain Wedding by Faye Gibbons

The Owl and the Pussycat by Edward Lear

Piggins and the Royal Wedding by Jane Yolen

The Rabbit's Wedding by Garth Williams

Rooster Who Went to His Uncle's Wedding by Alma Ada

Snapshots from the Wedding by Gary Soto

A Sweetheart for Valentine by Lorna Balian

Zoo Prop Box

Vocabulary

admission
amphibian
aviary
bear
bird
climate
concession stand
conservation
docent
elephant
enclosure
endangered
extinct
giraffe
habitat
kangaroo
mammal
monkey
nursery
panda
petting zoo
primate
refreshments
reptile
seal
sea lion
snake
tiger
visitor
zebra
zookeeper

Basic Props

Animal masks (teacher-made or commercial) (See directions in
   Appendix, page 120.)
Cash register or cash drawer
Corn or rice to feed the animals
Hats for zookeepers (old baseball caps)
Play money
Signs with animal names
Stuffed animals
Teacher-made badges for zookeepers
Zoo admission tickets
Zoo maps (obtained free at zoo)
Zoo signs
Zookeeper uniforms (adult shirts, white or blue)

Additional Props

Animal puzzles
Artificial rocks and plants
Audiotapes of animal sounds
Brooms to clean cages
Dolls and strollers
Overturned laundry baskets for cages
Plastic zoo figures
Textured animal fabrics
Zoo posters

Note: Veterinarian prop box can be combined with Zoo prop box
to provide materials for zoo veterinarians.

Extension Activities

- Take a field trip to the zoo. Find habitats that resemble the four basic shapes: square, circle, triangle, and rectangle.
- Watch the video *Zoo Crew: What Do You Want to Be When You Grow Up?*
- Discuss animal habitats with the children (forests, jungles, oceans, deserts, grasslands, mountains, savannah, and polar).
- Create zoo snacks by building animal cages with pretzels, peanut butter, and graham crackers. Place an animal cookie in the cage.
- Give children animal stickers and ask them to draw the animal's habitat.
- Use small plastic fruit baskets turned over as cages, and have children place a certain number of small plastic zoo animals in each cage.

- Discuss the meaning of extinction. Explain how human beings can help preserve the animal population.
- With the help of zoo personnel, have the class adopt an animal on the verge of extinction and help support its care.

Related Literature

Alligator Baby
  by Robert Munsch
Animals at the Zoo, on the Loose Too by Judith Lowe
Good Night, Gorilla
  by Peggy Rathmann
The Great Snake Escape
  by Molly Coxe
If Anything Ever Goes Wrong at the Zoo by Mary Jean Hendrick
If I Ran the Zoo by Dr. Seuss
Last Night at the Zoo
  by Michael Garland
A Lion Named Shirley Williamson by Bernard Waber
Lunch at the Zoo: What Animals Eat and Why
  by Joyce Ahman
Polar Bear, Polar Bear, What Do You Hear? by Bill Martin, Jr.
Put Me in the Zoo
  by Robert Lopshire
The Zoo at Night
  by Michael Rosen
Zoo Dreams by Cor Hazelaar
Zoo-Looking by Mem Fox

Appendix

Props

(Involve children in as many prop-making activities in this book as possible.)

Air Tanks

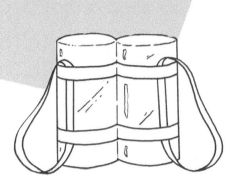

Cover two full rolls of paper towels or two half-gallon jugs with silver paper or aluminum foil. Tie them together with string so they lay side by side. Slide a cord or a couple of old belts lengthwise through the ties to act as shoulder straps. A short length of rubber hose may be attached to the air tanks by slipping one end under the cords holding the rolls together.

Animal Ear Headbands

Draw and color animal ears (bear, pig, wolf, and so on) on sturdy cardboard. Cut out and glue onto plastic headbands with a glue gun. (Tape is not recommended as it can catch in children's hair.)

Animal Masks

Masks are made easily from paper plates or by adding materials to commercial eye masks. When using paper plates, cut holes for eyes, nose, and mouth. Add animal features such as yarn for a lion's mane, feathers for a bird, or spots for a leopard. Attach string to paper plate masks so they can be tied on, or glue to a tongue depressor to be held in front of the face. Add ears, noses, or beaks; whiskers made from pipe cleaners; and hair made from yarn, dried moss, or cotton to commercial eye masks. Make beaks by cutting out an equilateral triangle, folding it in half, and gluing it to the mask. Make leopard faces by gluing or coloring spots on the mask and adding ears. Make tiger faces by drawing stripes on the mask.

ATM Machine

Use a medium-sized cardboard box for an ATM machine. Cut out a panel from one side of the box. This will allow a child to hide behind the ATM machine and serve as the "banker" for the machine. Cover the rest of the box with plain paper. On the opposite side of the cutout panel, draw the ATM window components. At the top of the panel, draw a rectangle and print "Welcome to _____ Bank" in the window. Below this window draw a square. In this square print the options for banking, such as "withdrawal" or "deposit." Cut two slots to the right of this panel. One slot is used for the bankcard. Below this slot, cut a larger slot for deposit and withdrawal of money. When a child uses the ATM machine, the child behind the machine serving as banker will receive and return the bankcard, as well as receive or give out cash through the slots in the panel. Place this box on a table.

Bakers' Hats

Cut an 8" x 22" rectangle out of white poster board. Wrap the long side of this rectangle around a child's head to form a cylinder. Tape or staple it to fit. (If you use staples, staple from the inside out to prevent children's hair from catching in the ends of the staples.) Tape or staple white tissue paper or sheeting fabric to the top to simulate a chef's hat.

Binoculars

Glue the sides of two toilet paper rolls together. Spray paint these "binoculars" black. Punch holes in both sides and tie an 18-20" cord or shoelace through the holes.

Breathing Apparatus

Punch six to eight holes just beneath the rim of a clear, eight-ounce plastic drinking cup. Thread a 14" length of thin elastic through two holes on opposite sides of the cup. Tie knots in both ends of the elastic. The elastic can be adjusted to hold the breathing apparatus in place. Extra holes will help air circulate inside the cup.

Cake

Use boxes or Styrofoam shapes as the cake form. (These can be a drum or box shape.) To make a cake with tiers, glue several forms on top of each other. Spray paint and decorate by gluing on button, rickrack, and fabric trim. Styrofoam may shred, but because it is porous children can poke candles into it. Holes to accommodate candles can also be punched in a cake made from boxes.

Campfire

Use 8 to 10 very small logs (approximately 12" long) or paint an equivalent number of paper towel rolls brown. If using real wood, be sure there are no splinters. Provide strips of red, yellow, and/or orange cellophane or tissue paper so children can build and start their own "fire."

Cricket Habitat

Clean and remove labels from two clear 2-liter soda bottles. Punch air holes in the bottles with an ice pick. Cut off 2" from the mouth of each bottle. With a box cutter, cut and remove the bottoms of the bottles following the contour of the bottle. Save the bottom pieces. Attach the two bottles at the mouths with duct tape. Lay the bottles down lengthwise. On the bottom of one bottle, place sticks, leaves, sand, and rocks. In the other bottle, place a small lid with drinking water, some sand, and a few tiny pieces of fruit and grain. Place the cricket in one of the bottles and reattach the bottoms of both bottles with duct tape to close up the bottles. You now have a cricket habitat. The cricket will walk back and forth between the bottles.

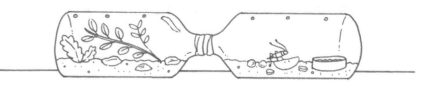

Director's "Take" Prop

Cut out two 2" x 8" rectangles and one 2" x 4" rectangle from sturdy cardboard. Paint them black and write "Action" on both sides of one long rectangle. Place the long rectangles together lengthwise. Place the short rectangle on top of one end. Use brass fasteners to connect the three rectangles.

Drive-up Window

Use a large cardboard storage box (refrigerator box is ideal). Cut out a window on one side of the box. Remove the opposite panel of the box so a child can sit behind or in the box to act as the banker. Cover the rest of the box with plain paper. Over the window, print the name of the bank. Cover an oatmeal container with plain paper. This can be used as the vacuum transfer tube to "send" deposits to the banker, similar to drive-up window vacuum tubes used by adults.

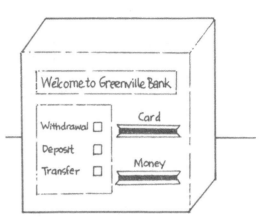

Firefighter Hats

On one half of a large piece of sturdy black construction paper, trace a large letter "U" approximately the width of a child's head. Insert the point of the scissors into the beginning of one of the legs of the U. Cut the legs of the U in one continuous cut. Lift the U forward and crease so the U stands up. This is the top and front of the hat. Draw an emblem here. Trim the corners of the hat so they are more rounded.

Goldilocks' Wig

Use a girl's hat as a form for the wig. Glue lengths of thick yellow or gold yarn onto the hat with a glue gun. If using a hat with a brim, glue the yarn around the hat band. (If desired, make thick braids from the yarn before attaching to the hat.)

Gurney (or Stretcher)

Use a large bath towel or a piece of cloth cut into a rectangular shape. Cut two pieces of ½" dowel so they are 12" longer than the towel lengthwise. Fold the towel edges over and sew or staple in place, making a tube to push the dowels through. (Make sure the fold is large enough to accommodate the width of the dowel.) Place the dowels on either side of the towel so the dowels stick out beyond the towel evenly on both ends. This will form the handles of the stretcher.

back

Hard Hat with Bear Ears

Draw and color bear ears on sturdy cardboard. Cut out ears, leaving a ½" wide tab along the bottom of the ears. To make ears stand up, cut a flap in the tab that can be bent in the opposite direction from the rest of the tab. Use a glue gun to attach the ear tabs onto a child-sized hat.

Instrument or Space Control Panel

Cover a piece of heavy-duty cardboard (cut from a packing box or a small tri-fold display board) with aluminum foil or spray paint it silver. Glue on spools and plastic milk bottle lids. Glue on drawings or photographs of a speedometer, clock, and a "view" from the window.

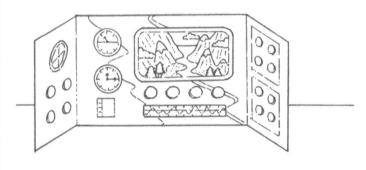

Jester Hat

Stuff four or five brightly colored socks with newspaper. Sew the cuffs of the socks shut. Attach bells to the ends of each sock with hot glue or thread. Sew the socks in a circle onto an old baseball cap, a knitted winter hat, or any other type of hat. Attach chin ties to the hat, or the weight of the socks will cause the hat to fall off.

Knight's Helmet

Cut off the top of a one-gallon plastic milk jug. Turn the jug upside down so the opening is on the bottom. Cut two holes for the eyes and a rectangular opening for the mouth. Spray paint silver or cover with aluminum foil. Attach a feather or other decoration to the top.

Magician's Hat

On black paper trace the widest part of a half-gallon circular ice cream container. Draw another circle 2" wider around this circle to make a brim for the hat. Cut out the brim. Cover the ice cream container with black paper. Attach the brim of the hat to the open part of the container, forming a top hat children can wear or use for tricks.

Microphone

Paint a toilet paper roll black. Glue a Ping-Pong ball or Styrofoam ball of similar size to one end of the paper roll.

Milking a Cow

Place two chairs of equal height back to back, leaving a couple of feet of space between them. Place a wooden rod across the top of the two chairs. Prick holes in the fingertips of a rubber glove. Attach the wrist of the rubber glove to the middle of the rod with string with the fingers hanging down. Leave a small opening to allow you to fill the glove with water. Place a pail under the glove. Fill the glove with water using a funnel. Children pretend they are milking the cow by pulling on the fingers of the rubber glove.

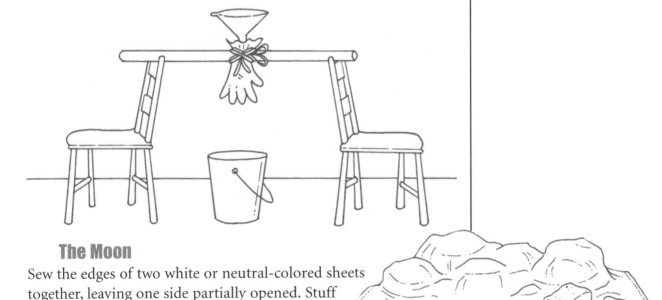

The Moon

Sew the edges of two white or neutral-colored sheets together, leaving one side partially opened. Stuff this large "pillow" loosely with enough scrap foam to create a bouncy surface. Stitch the opening closed.

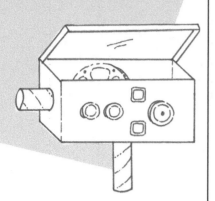

Movie Camera

Find a sturdy, hinged shoebox. (Spray paint if there is too much writing on it.) Place the box on a table so the hinge is on the top right side. Cut circular openings the same size as paper towel rolls in the bottom and in the "front" (the side farthest away) of the box. Wedge the rolls into each opening and cut them to the right length. The roll in the bottom is the camera's handle. The roll in the front is the camera's lens. Once adjusted, glue in place. Draw camera features on the outside and inside of the camera. (For example, draw a film reel inside the camera.) Glue on button and bottle lids. Cut an opening in the side opposite the lens so children can look through the camera.

Octopus

Cut off the legs of old pantyhose (4 pairs to make 8 legs) and stuff with newspaper or Styrofoam packing peanuts. Tie the pantyhose legs to an old belt, making sure they are evenly spaced. Tie the belt around a child's waist to make an octopus.

Pompom Yarn Balls

Cut two identical cardboard circles about 2" in diameter. Cut out a ½" diameter circle in the center of these two circles so they look like doughnuts. Place one circle on top of the other so the centers are lined up. Cut two 3' lengths of yarn and a 9" length of yarn. Hold the end of the 3' piece of yarn with your thumb pressed against the circle. With your other hand, push the yarn through the center of the circles and begin to wrap the yarn around the cardboard doughnuts, making sure the strands are close together and tight. You may need to use both 3-foot pieces of yarn to completely cover the circles. When the circles are covered with yarn, hold the center of the circles firmly with the fingers of one hand. With the other hand, insert the tip of a pair of scissors between the two cardboard circles and cut the yarn apart at the outer edge of the circles, carefully turning the cardboard as you go along. Do not let go of the yarn and the circles. When all the strands have been cut, take the 9" length of yarn and insert it between the two pieces of cardboard, pull tight and tie firmly. Pull the cardboard pieces off the yarn ball. Slap the ball against your palm to fluff it up.

Princess Hat

Use a cone-shaped paper party hat or cut a stiff piece of colored cardboard into a triangle shape and roll it into a cone. Punch a hole into either side of the bottom of the cone and attach ribbons or string to tie the hat under the chin. Cut different lengths of ribbon or crepe paper streamers and glue or staple the streamers to the pointed end of the cone. A long piece of sheer fabric can also be used in place of streamers or ribbon. Attach the fabric to the point of the cone with hot glue or staples.

"Red Light, Green Light"

This is a variation of the traditional game of "Red Light, Green Light." Use chalk to draw a runway on the blacktop or cement on the playground. This can be a series of parallel dotted lines or a wide solid line. One child is chosen to be the air traffic controller. The rest of the children are pilots. The air traffic controller stands at one end of the runway in the "control tower." The pilots line up on the other end. When the air traffic controller calls, "Green light," the pilots "taxi" along the runway with their arms outstretched. When the air traffic controller calls, "Red light," the pilots must stop immediately. If a pilot does not stop on this signal, he or she must return to the beginning of the runway. The first pilot to reach the control tower becomes the next air traffic controller.

Royal Scepter

Spray a dowel that is ¼" in diameter and 1½' long with gold spray paint. Cut out a star or use a Ping-Pong ball and attach the star or ball to one end of the dowel. The star can be hot glued, and the ball can be attached by making a small hole in the ball and slipping it onto the end of the dowel with a dab of hot glue. Cover the star or ball with glitter. Tie different lengths of ribbon to the end of the scepter after attaching the star or ball.

Space Helmets

Cut a gallon-size plastic milk container in half. On one side, cut out a semicircle large enough to accommodate a child's face. Spray paint it silver or white. Make sure the corners are rounded and cover all sharp edges with duct tape. Use a permanent marker to write NASA on the helmet.

Submarine

Place a large cardboard box (for example, a refrigerator box) on its side. Leave one end open so children can climb in. On one side of the box, cut out round portholes and cover them with blue cellophane to create an underwater illusion. Cut out a large rectangle at one end of the box for the front window of the submarine and cover with blue cellophane. Spray paint the submarine silver. Inside the box on the front wall of the submarine, draw dials and control mechanisms. Dials may be attached to the box using bottle caps and brads so children can turn the dials. Suspend colorful fish cutouts on string outside the portholes.

Toy Stick Horses

Cut a wooden dowel 3' long and 1" in diameter. Stuff a brown, black, or white adult sock tightly with newspaper. This is the horse's head. Cut yarn strips 6" long. Sew or hot glue these yarn lengths along the ankle part of the sock to create the horse's mane. Sew one button on each side of the sock foot, which is the horse's nose, to make the eyes. Braid three lengths of yarn or use a length of strong side ribbon to make the bridles. Loop this over the horse's nose and attach to both sides of the face with thread or hot glue. With a marker or paint, draw a mouth and two nostrils on the horse's face. Insert the dowel into the open end of the sock and tie the sock onto the dowel by wrapping yarn or string tightly around the sock. You can also staple the horse's head to the dowel with a staple gun.

Wizard's Hat

Trace a wedge on a piece of purple or black tag board. Roll the wedge shape into a cone shape. Punch a hole on either side of the bottom of the cone and attach ribbons or string to tie the hat under the chin. Cover the hat with star-shaped stickers. Using a variety of sizes of stars makes the hat more interesting.

Bubble Solution

¼ cup liquid laundry or dishwashing detergent
½ cup water
1 teaspoon sugar

Mix ingredients. Use traditional bubble wands to blow bubbles or experiment with alternative bubble wands made from six-pack can holders, strawberry baskets, small mesh strainers, or telephone or electrical wire bent into wand shapes.

Oobleck (Monster Mud)

5 parts cornstarch
5 parts water
food coloring

Add food coloring to water. Mix in cornstarch a little at a time until mixture can be picked up in your hands and will slowly ooze through your fingers. If it gets too thick while in use, add more water. If it is too runny, let it settle and then pour off the water that rises to the top.

Playdough

2 cups water
food coloring
2 cups flour
1 cup salt
½ cup cornstarch
2 tablespoons vegetable oil
1 tablespoon powdered alum or cream of tartar (as a preservative)

Add food coloring to water. Mix all ingredients in a medium-sized pan. Cook over medium heat, stirring constantly, until thick. Remove from pan and knead until smooth. Makes about 3 cups.

(If covered tightly, this playdough will keep for weeks.)

Trail Mix

Combine equal parts of:
raisins or other dried fruit
nuts
pretzels
chocolate chips
chex-type cereal
granola

Pay close attention to children's food allergies, especially nuts, before selecting ingredients.

Book Index

Index